Today's business world is super competitive and unforgiving and career growth is more often than not, a perilous journey. *The McKinsey Edge* is absolutely terrific. It provides a wealth of knowledge and practical tools to help you stand-out among your peers and to amplify your career.

—JAMES HUANG
VICE PRESIDENT, CHANNELADVISOR
CORPORATION

Among the plethora of books about leadership, this book stands out by its sheer practicality. As a very readable combination of leadership principles, insights from famous people and the author's own intriguing day-to-day experiences at McKinsey, this book is required reading for any aspiring future business leader.

—DR. LUDWIG KANZLER
FORMER MCKINSEY PARTNER

As a former McKinsey consultant, I found Hattori's book to be a nostalgic walk through memory lane. At the same time, I was struck by how just many of the concepts captured have been instrumental to my leadership development. *The McKinsey Edge* provides the right mix of the theoretical and practical, and is well suited to students of business as well as managers at all levels.

—STANFORD LIN
HEAD OF PRODUCTS FOR VISA CHINA,
FORMER MCKINSEY CONSULTANT

THE McKINSEY EDGE

THE McKINSEY EDGE

Success Principles from the World's Most Powerful Consulting Firm

SHU HATTORI

New York Chicago San Francisco Athens London Madrid
Mexico City Milan New Delhi Singapore Sydney Toronto

1 2 3 4 5 6 7 8 9 0   DOC/DOC   1 2 1 0 9 8 7 6 5

ISBN   978-1-259-58868-6
MHID   1-259-58868-8

e-ISBN   978-1-259-58299-8
e-MHID   1-259-58299-X

Library of Congress Cataloging-in-Publication Data

Hattori, Shu
    The McKinsey edge : success principles from the world's most powerful consulting firm / Shu Hattori.
        pages cm
    Includes bibliographical references.
    ISBN 978-1-259-58868-6 (alk. paper) — ISBN 1-259-58868-8 (alk. paper) 1. Success in business. 2. Management. 3. Leadership. 4. Consulting firms—Management—Case studies. I. Title.
    HF5386.H277 2016
    658.4'09--dc23   2015028853

McGraw-Hill Education books are available at special quantity discounts to use as premiums and sales promotions or for use in corporate training programs. To contact a representative, please visit the Contact Us pages at www.mhprofessional.com.

To Carmen, my source of love and inspiration.

If it weren't for you, I wouldn't be here.

Kaz and Noriko, who are everything a child dreams.

And, Tomo, who told me to live in the moment.

CONTENTS

CHAPTER TWO
Growing with Others 63

ACKNOWLEDGMENTS

I had written most of this book unknowingly over the years. Then it took another intense one year and a half (outside the Firm) to further synthesize, clean up and come up with more meaning and implications. It started with a suggestion—that I publish this. Then it became a wish. I wished something like this existed for me when I was learning: short, handy and practical. Then it became a reality. I was fortunately able to find a publisher who also liked this idea.

Aside from my own wisdom I learned at McKinsey, I sought wonderful advice from talented individuals. At the onset, I wanted the interviews to distill what I had learned and give a richer sense of what was more important. Then as the interviews grew and details ensued, I truly found that these principles were converging. I had somehow hit a plateau around 40 to 50. Every time I added beyond that, the principles weren't as forthcoming and concentrated. The more I carried the discussion forward, the more I realized that the sweet number rested somewhere in between.

I am grateful for the countless number of meetings, interviews, and on-the-job coaching with the following individuals: (in alphabetical order, McKinsey people are denoted with an asterisk)

Peter Bradd, Diane Ducarme,* Tim Fountaine,* Tina Hou,* Ulrich Huber,* James Huang, Laurent Kinet,* Genki Oka,* Rajesh Parekh,* Felix Poh,* Dave Rogers,* Tak Sakamoto,* Jeongmin Seong,* Kai Shen,* Roi Shigematsu,* Jonathan Woetzel,* Hagen Wulferth,* Karen Yeoh, Forrest Zhang,* and Chanqing Zheng.* Others who gave me inspiration over the years include Wouter Aghina,* Gwen Blandin,* Kimberly Borden,* Jason Chen,* Nao Iwatani,* Davis Lin,* Robert Mathis,* Derrick Miu, Hyosoo Park,* Philipp Radtke,* and Bill Wiseman.*

I cannot express in words how much you each have given me in terms of time and intellectual wisdom. Your support and thoughts enabled me to crystallize a much more refined end product. There are a few people I want to give special thanks to: Jeongmin, for giving me invaluable advice on structuring. Also, "Who else should I introduce for you?" really gave me the strengths to know I had one big supporter. Diane, for brainstorming, slicing and dicing, many different principles. Also, "Do you want to take this paper with you?" as I almost forgot on many occasions. Tim, for spending an incredibly long morning discussing leadership in Sydney. Tim, I don't know if I can be your book mentor, but I am happy to talk about it, anytime (I am not revealing your secret idea to anyone, yet).

I also would like to thank my McGraw-Hill editor, Knox Huston, who did a superb job in guiding me in spite of all the time differences. Also, for taking me through the nuts and bolts of writing a compelling book. I wanted to be structured as much as possible, and you helped accommodate that.

I want to also thank my early readers: Yoon-Suk Choo and Derrick Miu. Yoon, without your candid and timely feedback, I would have never been able to get past the first milestone. Thank you for also helping me throughout the entire process, including the legal advice. It was indeed a fabulous journey, don't you think? I couldn't have done it without you. Derrick, thanks for your warm words of encouragement. You inspire me to do better. Thank you both for being my best and ideal friends.

Finally, I couldn't have even fathomed this project without my wife Carmen. I am forever in your debt. This has been one of my long-term aspirations, and I am so fortunate to have such a loving and thoughtful partner. To my mom and dad: thanks for letting me stay over at your sweet home in Hamamatsu while I refocused my attention. You both make me believe that I can do anything with this life. My thanks also go out to my brother, Tomo, for spiritual support (I think my long journey all started with your, "Take this and just go to Taiwan" back in 2004), and David Roff, his best friend and author, who, by sharing his experience on book writing, encouraged me to give it a try. I would also like to thank Christy, Tom, Fengyang, and Xiumei for cheering me on.

To all the locations that inspired me while on this incredible journey: Tokyo, San Francisco, Toronto, New York, Taipei, Shanghai, Sydney, and Queensland. Thanks!

Lastly, good luck!

INTRODUCTION

How It Came to Be

There are people in this world who are born gifted. They have photographic memory or they remember things for a lifetime after hearing them only once. These people may not need to rely on written principles. They absorb everything like sponges.

I am the opposite. I need to jot everything down. From general feedback sessions to pointers in meetings to keynote speech phrases to interesting frameworks, I write everything down. I also try to invent different diagrams to make the visualization and memorization easier. I keep two notebooks, in fact. One is a clean and tidy one—learning purpose. The other is more scribbly and disorganized—daily purpose. Generally speaking, people learn by studying. Then they put what they've studied (their knowledge) into practice. Practice leads to experience. More experience leads to ability. Ability is the final stage where you have mastered something that no one can take away from you.

I entered McKinsey (known as "the Firm") in April 2008 as a business analyst. I made it to the next level by June 2010, a direct-to-associate (DTA) promotion at the Firm. Then I transferred offices and left for Groupon.com in Asia, the fastest-growing social commerce company at the time, as one of the management executives. There my salary tripled in less than a year to a high six-figure salary.

But then I came upon an idea of a secret wedding proposal business and founded my own company. It attracted local TV and magazine attention in six months. It was one and only, occupying a unique niche market. But, after a year and a half, I realized I still wanted to go back to McKinsey. I felt that I had not finished learning the nitty-gritty details of project management at the world's best place for professional leadership. In less than a year after rejoining, I made engagement manager in record time. It was a combination of determination and luck—or that was what I believed until the winter of 2013.

One chilly morning, I was sitting in the Firm's office canteen going over my learning notebook, or the "rulebook," brushing phrases up, cleaning diagrams, and making "synthesized rules" from my past project (aka engagement). I liked the peace and quiet of the moment, sitting in a comfortable lounge chair and soaking up the morning sunlight. A colleague stopped over and asked me what I was doing, so I told him. Then he raised my notebook and his eyebrows at the same time. My colleague was amazed and suggested I publish my writing. It was the first time I'd let anyone see it. Until that point, I'd always imagined everyone to be doing the same thing.

Initially I was a bit hesitant. I didn't know if it was deep enough. Then slowly, as I started going over my notebook, I thought maybe his suggestion wasn't so strange. It seemed like a very good reason to write a book—to share all the pieces of wisdom that I had collected during my time at McKinsey.

As this new project started taking shape, I also sought out other amazing colleagues for advice. I thought, "What if they also had two or three burning rules that made them extremely successful on their roads to leadership?" As expected, many had a few golden rules they kept close at heart. Now, I was sure that I could create immense value in what I was about to produce.

In hindsight, the learning notebook was my reason for success. Unknowingly, it enabled me to correct mistakes faster, preempt potential roadblocks, and get ahead of the learning curve. Simply, it elevated me to a leadership position and got me thinking faster. In a more general sense, the notebook told me not only what to do but *how to do it.*

By reading this book, hopefully, you can gain the same benefits. What is important is that you put what you learn into use immediately. I always try to put my rules into action the following day or at the next opportunity that comes around. Try to focus on what matters to you (the first principle of the book is "Focus on What Really Matters") now and rigorously put it into practice. It's probably not possible to master all of the principles at once. Create a plan and go batches at a time. Lastly, keep in mind that practice equals experience, which leads to ability in the long run.

Why Should You Listen?

McKinsey loves leaders.

But, as the old saying goes, "Leaders are never born, they're made."

Before joining the Firm, I used to wonder why so many people from consulting firms, especially from firms like McKinsey, made it to the top. Let me tell you some numbers I found. Did you know that according to *USA Today* the odds of a McKinsey alumnus becoming a CEO of a publicly traded company of market value over $2 billion are the highest in the world, at 1 in 690? The runner-up didn't even come close—at 1 in 2,150 (also another consulting firm). In 2011, 150 McKinsey alumni had top spots in companies with annual sales of over $1 billion. Not to mention that 70 McKinsey alumni have been CEOs of Fortune 500 companies in recent years, according to *CNBC*, which cited Duff McDonald, a New York–based journalist and contributing editor for *Fortune* magazine.

McKinsey is considered a CEO launchpad by many aspiring leaders.[1]

After joining the Firm, McKinsey consultants go through a wide array of leadership training events. These week-long training events start very early, beginning 9 to 12 months after a consultant joins the Firm. Then they repeat almost every year for the next decade. The emphasis is not merely on teaching different types of tools, processes, and problem-solving techniques for leaders but on engraining the *awareness of leadership* early on. Ultimately, I have learned that the biggest obstacle for many people is that they are not sufficiently self-actualized to realize that they could become leaders. McKinsey sets different forms of leadership out on the table early on: "client leadership," "problem-solving leadership," "team leadership," "knowledge or functional leadership," and "entrepreneurial leadership" to help consultants build strengths and discover weaknesses (McKinsey calls it "development needs") faster. These different categories of leadership are helpful because they slice the necessary individual growth attributes in a meaningful and simple-to-understand way.

One common stereotype of a leader is someone who can stand up on stage and deliver a captivating speech, or who is calm and composed in times of crisis, or who is willing to go out of his or her way to help others. These are important qualities, but there's really no one way of defining what makes a good leader. Take Apple for example. Tim Cook, the successor of Steve Jobs, is not a particularly inspiring public speaker. He is a steadfast operations guru with his calm demeanor to push things through. Steve Jobs, needless to say, was the visionary pitchman. Since Jobs's passing, Apple's behemoth market cap has continued to grow, almost doubling,*

---

* On October 4, 2011, a day before Steve Jobs's passing, Apple's market cap was at $346 billion; on November 26, 2014, it was $698 billion (highest in the past five years). To put this into perspective, Google's market cap on November 26, 2014, was at $367 billion and Microsoft was $394 billion.

with a very different and unique leadership profile.[2] According to many McKinsey consultants, engagement managers and principals alike, it's hardly the case that they meet principals and directors that are very similar to one another.

Leaders come in different colors. Some leaders don't like to speak in front of a large audience but still do a great job on the line. Therefore, you are better off if you are exposed to many different types of leaders during your apprenticeship years. This is one of the reasons why McKinsey consultants can grow to be prominent leaders (recall 1 in 690)—almost every project consultant gets to work with different internal senior leaders and client executives.

The Hardest Transition

For a lot of people, the associate to engagement manager transition is the most challenging and unforgettable experience. It's no secret. "My first study as an engagement manager was literally a nightmare," a senior director said in an interview. "I was staffed on a transportation client with an ED (engagement director) who absolutely had too much on his hands, an associate who was a bit of a psychopath, and another associate who wouldn't listen to a word I said. I was this first-time manager and struggling to keep everyone alive. Even after so many years, the experience brings back so many horrifying memories," he laughed. Another principal said, "My first study was memorable. I had an associate that was a bit off. When I told him to come back with some synthesis on past interviews, he came back with 50 one-line syntheses of all the interviews. When I saw that, I just knew my weekend was blown. It wasn't that he lacked a good mindset; instead, he was just off, if you know what I mean." These stories are not uncommon. For the first time in many people's lives they were (like it or not) in full charge of everything and helplessly out of control at the same time. From end output deliverables to designing optimal work processes, from assigning meaningful tasks to helping individuals stay personally motivated, from thinking day in and day out about client needs (as one other director puts it, "Even in the shower!") to taking on rapid-fire update inputs from senior leaders—it was overwhelming. There was no hiding behind anyone's shoulders. You had to be the first person to walk in the team room and the last one to go. People looked to you for directions, and it had to be "ready and practical." But like most first timers, the experience takes a steep nosedive at first. As a result, the survivor learns the survival tactics. But more important, according to many senior executive leaders and McKinsey principals and directors, the foundational leadership principles stick with you and stay consistent until you reach the top. You will see plenty of these examples in this book.

Structure of the Book

This book is structured into five main sections.

Building the Self, as the name suggests, focuses on self-improvement. The section is split into three thematic areas: Get Ahead, Hang Tight, and Multiple Reflections. There are many interesting mini-themes throughout the book. But the core of personal victory boils down to a few simple things. You need to think ahead. You need ways to deal with tough times. You need to have a heart to reflect more so you can optimize your future success.

Growing with Others focuses on how to influence your team and other stakeholders. Leadership transition is learning on one hand your growth needs but on the other hand, and more important, stakeholders' needs. The three important themes here are communication, connection, and understanding. When you want your team members to grow, the key is to put in more effort than you would normally give for yourself. This is how hard you should work at growing others.

Excelling in Process Management is about productivity themes. I've managed to include a few enablers—tools that help you structure and complement your current work process. In becoming a highly structured and process-driven person, it's important to execute the basics right. That is why you will see overly intuitive principles at first glance. Yet, as the saying goes, "Most [seemingly] simple things are the most difficult to execute."

Going the Extra Mile, the fourth chapter, focuses on six advanced principles. They require deliberation. The last two, *Prepare to Renew Your Life* and *Start to Create Your Own "Profile" as a Leader*, are especially important throughout your entire career. You will need to develop these thoughts as early as possible but also be ready to change them along the way.

Become a Thinker and a Writer, the fifth and final chapter, ties all the principles together into a single theme: Thinking Sets Leaders Apart. Enrich your world by asking the how and why questions. Then, as a way to internalize your thinking, put these thoughts on paper. Marvin Bower, the founding father of management consulting, says good writing empowers you to distill and crystallize your thoughts.

The success principles in this book should not be hard to put in practice. (If they were, it would mean I did not do a good job explaining them.) The correct way to think is that these principles are immediately implementable from tomorrow, but each principle will take time to develop into an actual ability. The general thought framework I have used is to first describe what each principle is, then why it's important, how it should be done, and when, where, or in what situations it may be most applicable. A master coach with over two decades of experience coaching top executives once told me that accomplishing great things requires "setting an extremely *low* bar" so that it is easily attainable at first. For example, instead of saying you will go exercise five times a week to lose weight, just say you will go once a week. If even this sounds difficult, then say, I will go walking once a week instead of taking the cab or subway on my way home from work, and so on. It's the incremental move that is important, he stressed. Therefore, these principles should be *managed* the same way. Take small steps to make the giant leadership leap in the end.

Now, let the curtain rise!

CHAPTER ONE

Building the Better Self

*There's a difference between knowing the path and walking the path.**

—MORPHEUS, FROM THE MATRIX

This chapter, focuses on fundamental self-improvement. Contrary to the typical approach to improvement—fixating on just your faults and weaknesses and remedying them as you go along—the principles here focus on a more proactive approach. This way you can maximize your strengths. Until I reached a certain level of maturity, I used to think of growth as a random journey. It may fortunately work for some but not for others. But later I realized it's a lot better if you can create your own structure and rigor for self-improvement.

For me, that rigor is in three areas, which I call get ahead, hang tight, and multiple reflections.

---

* In the 1999 blockbuster megahit movie *The Matrix*, directed by the Wachowskis, Morpheus (Laurence Fishburne) tells Neo (Keanu Reeves) that knowing the path is different from walking the path, when Neo tries to tell him the truth about not being the chosen "one." This phrase told me (then 17 years of age) that over life, the necessary effort it would take to get what I wanted, even if I had all the blessings and knew the A to Z on how to get there, would not only be hard and tough but also extraordinary and unimaginable.

Get Ahead

In "get ahead" there are six principles. Below, I have synthesized the core messages in one line.

PRINCIPLE 1
Focus on What Really Matters. Constantly have a razor-sharp awareness of what you are doing and how it is adding value to you or to your problems.

PRINCIPLE 2
Start with the Hard Stuff in the Morning. Work on the hard and painful tasks in the morning to deliver productive output.

PRINCIPLE 3
Catch Small Signals and Make a Difference. Apply the Pareto analysis or 80-20 rule to your everyday life.

PRINCIPLE 4
Have a 30-Second Answer to Everything. Form an answer beforehand by mastering the "double-clicking" technique and coming up with short answers.

PRINCIPLE 5
Frontload Your Project. Build the necessary trust and credibility by completing work as much as possible during the first week, following the basket of essentials.

PRINCIPLE 6
Create the Right End Output Image. Try to get in the habit of creating the end output image aggressively to earn various stakeholders' trust early on.

PRINCIPLE 1 Focus on What Really Matters

McKinsey charts are not very colorful. The text size is the same throughout except for the title. The fonts follow either the client's format or Times New Roman, and footnotes follow a specific rule. Graphs and diagrams also have standardized templates. One chart, one message, one format. Nothing fancy. It's because we want the recipient to focus on one thing: the implication. Everything else will deter this effort. McKinsey consultants are extremely careful over a single word or a phrase because that really matters.

To a CEO, numbers matter most. Mark Hurd, co-CEO of Oracle Corporation, said he learned from his boss at NCR, a global company in consumer transaction technologies, that it doesn't matter how gracefully you deliver a presentation. In the end, if your numbers "suck," there's not much to say. His best advice is to focus on "underlying substance."[1]

Almost everyone who enters the Firm's gate relearns what he or she has previously learned and been proud of back in MBA training or in other companies regarding how to draw charts. Instead of catchy and animated callouts, they learn to use a blank callout text box with an arrow pointed to a "manlike figure" made up of a circle and an isosceles triangle. Rather than using size 12 and 24 fonts to accentuate an important point, the entire page is reduced to an even font of 14. They no longer use green text to show that something is good to go but instead a green traffic light made up of three circles aligned vertically. Everyone picks up the essence of what's important on a chart.

As you transcend or think about the next leadership horizon, you need to focus on what really matters for that position. At McKinsey, you go through a course specifically targeted to build "problem-solving leaders." Here we learn about staying ahead of the problem and leading by bringing together different stakeholders. In this position, we often get asked by principals and directors,

"Can you update me on the current status?" This is another way of saying, "Tell me what really matters on this project in 30 seconds." Therefore, it's imperative to synthesize and regularly play back in your head the problem, the current solution, and the proposed approach in terms of milestones, people, and timeline.

What really matters can be different from industry to industry. For the automotive industry, it's safety and design. For the pharmaceutical industry, it's the effectiveness of the drug, how fast it works, and how long it lasts. For a headhunting company, it's the candidate's average length of stay at his or her newly appointed jobs. For consulting, it's the message (so what?) and the estimated impact that implication brings—consultants arrive at this message and impact through following a series of problem-solving steps. In McKinsey's case, it involves: (1) identifying the problem, (2) structuring the problem (making sure all the issues are covered by using a MECE, mutually exclusive and collectively exhaustive, approach), (3) prioritizing and eliminating unnecessary problems, (4) creating the analysis and work plan, (5) conducting the analysis, (6) synthesizing to derive meaningful results, (7) delivering the right communication message. In the end, the message needs to be tailored to fit the client context (capability, resource, and execution power) to lead to any tangible impact. In many cases, it's possible to list out multiple things that matter, but the important thing is to distinguish what matters most to the problem at hand. For automotive, it may additionally be ergonomics, fuel efficiency, and product launch time *on top of* safety and design. For one client, the issue was how to build and finish a car in the next 36 months. Thus, what became the most important matter was product concept to launch time. The team accessed and analyzed the top five automakers' product launch schedules. The winner turned out to be Toyota with the shortest at 24 months—and the slowest was 40 months, a gap that is hard to believe! Logically, the next question became, why? It was attributable to the number of platforms each automaker had. Toyota had the fewest. It built most of its cars on the same platform, all around the globe. It forced the design to fit a particular platform mold and thereby eliminated the longer design concept to platform path. *That* knowledge for our client was gold. It was what really mattered.

When you focus your efforts on important cornerstone areas, other things start falling into place. Successful entrepreneurs say don't worry about what you're going to call your company. The right name will pop up once your product or service idea is on the verge of release. Yet, so many people still dwell on insignificant things like the name, logo, and how the business card will look. Those are important but less meaningful, especially in the beginning. Focusing on what really matters will help streamline your journey. In this case, focus on creating the core services of your business. Test them out. Iterate with as many people as you can. Challenge any doubts or premonitions you may have. Usually a clear alarm should go off when you hear yourself saying, "I will start on this when the business gets rolling." Ask immediately, "Can I do it now? Why not?" Then take the necessary incremental steps forward. Usually this will come in the form of decision making, closing outputs, or narrowing the solution space. Whether it's directly related to your work, personal projects, skill enhancement, health, or relationships, try to seek what matters most in that area all the time.

How might you accomplish this focus and prioritization? There are three ways to cut to the chase: (1) using the sense of urgency and deadline, (2) creating or following the critical path, and (3) linking it to the money.

First and easiest is to work on are the urgent items with tighter deadlines. In your head, without jotting anything down, you should roughly have the time it takes to complete a certain task. Although your estimate may be off at times, it is still a good place to start by eliminating those items that are far out into the future. When you do, take an objective stance. Consider the company logo, for example. It may seem important and urgent, but in reality it's not. These logos change all the time, and hence, you should just leave it alone for a while. Think Google. It really has no set logo and frequently changes its home search page look.

Second, understand the critical path to get to your goal. At McKinsey, during a marketing or branding study, we sometimes run an exercise called the consumer decision journey. This exercise tries to figure out where, how, and why consumers arrive at the decision to buy a particular product. We derive insights by gaining both an external and internal perspective of the target consumers. Externally, we run and analyze a consumer survey based on initial consideration, various online and offline touch points, timing of those interventions, consumer-led research, and other factors. Internally, we map out how the rational mind arrives at making such decisions, which we call the consumer decision tree. For example, if you were to buy a new TV, we would look at each of the five or six variables important to you as a consumer and rank them: price, brand, size, type (LCD/LED or OLED), and other functionalities such as HD. In this case, typically you will first think about the size of the TV. Then it splits to either price or brand, or you might adjust the size based on price and brand. These decisions are the branches of the "tree." When you consider what matters in any situation, it is important to keep this kind of decision tree in your mind.

Third, think about linking the task directly to its financial impact. This is the most straightforward yet remarkably precise method for most people. In other words, it's the key performance indicator (KPI) or the "meat" of what you are doing. For example, writers like to read. They also like to research. I sometimes get carried away and absorbed in—or distracted by, depending on how you look at it—some topic for an insane amount of my time. Yet, it is producing written content on paper that actually indicates prog-ress. It is the *only* way to reach the end product. Writers get paid to write. Thus, spending three hours on research and writing three sentences on paper means I didn't get much work done. It sounds intuitive, but a lot of us miss this point. Just like musicians need to produce music but may listen to other artists for inspiration, you should know what tasks directly link to the money. It is by far the most obvious way to focus on what really matters.

Even as you read this book, focus on principles that matter to you. It will be impossible to go through all of the principles at once. Try to tackle them one at a time focusing on building your core substance.

PRINCIPLE 2 Start with the Hard Stuff in the Morning

"The early bird catches the worm" is an old mantra that stands the test of time. Early morning hours are peaceful and quiet. It's the perfect time alone. Since most people are not out of bed yet, that makes you feel a bit proud. You pour yourself a nice cup of coffee and sit at your desk. "Ah," you say, "it's time to get some work done."

So the question is, "What work should you concentrate on in these early hours?"

The hard stuff. What's the hard stuff?

From your to-do list . . .
- It's the work you least want to do.
- It's the long result, not the low-hanging one.
- It's the work you usually say you'll do in the afternoon when you have a solid three or four hours to get a good bite at it.
- It's also work where you need full attention.
- It's the work that is painful.

- It's the work you know least how to tackle. Probably you need help. You need to launch it and think through.
- It's also work that later on, if you don't start early and delegate some of the tasks, you will be stuck doing all by yourself.

Here are some examples of the actual work:
- Writing your executive summary
- Creating work packages and timelines for the next three months
- Producing end output and goals
- Drafting important materials for a CEO or C-level executive workshop
- Giving new inputs to team members' work
- Drafting action e-mails

Generally speaking, it's work that requires invention, creation, and imagination.

It's not . . .
- Editing something
- Proofreading a document
- Adding a couple of additional support sentences or slides to your presentation
- Replying to e-mails or requests
- Menial tasks such as creating an e-mail contact list of all your project members

Generally speaking, it's not changing, fixing, or destroying something.

So when do you complete the more mundane but necessary work—the changing, fixing, or destroying work? At night! After a challenging day, you are usually quite exhausted by dinner. Even though it's quiet at night, you don't have the mental capacity to go over output from team and clients, focus on valuable work, raise difficult issues, do something creative, or think into the future. You just want to relax your brain. It's the best time to be engaged in the passive, less thinking-intensive work.

Creating a "get up early and go to sleep earlier" biorhythm will prove to be an important habit for you to transition into a mainstream leader. A quick look into the daily wake-up time of 21 notable CEOs revealed that 80 percent of them wake up before 6 A.M.[2] The earliest bird was Fiat and Chrysler CEO Sergio Machione waking at 3:30 A.M. to deal with his counterparts in the European market. Celebrity leaders Richard Branson of Virgin Group and Howard Schultz of Starbucks wake up at 5:45 and 5:00 A.M. respectively.* They both exercise first thing.

Now, think about your aspiring leaders. What time do they send around e-mails? A lot of them in early morning hours—except for those who ping you 24 hours a day, usually more in our line of work than elsewhere. On one project, the head of Aftersales was so busy during the day that I could only get a decent interaction going in these morning hours. He and I sat at 7:15 A.M. in the first-floor coffee shop to discuss rising inventory and back-order issues. It was by far the most efficient 30 minutes I've ever had. A couple of months back when I ran into him, he was still impressed at that maneuver, and just because of that one incident we became good friends. Lucky me! From an age standpoint, the younger you are, the more likely you will gain respect by waking up early and getting things done. We've all been there and know it's hard when you're young.

Second, getting up early to do the hard stuff makes sense from a scientific standpoint. Your body temperature usually fluctuates 0.5 C (0.9 F) during the day, with the lowest levels around 4 or 5 A.M.,

---

* Other CEOs and founders who wake up early include Tim Armstrong (AOL), Karen Blackett (MediaCom), Hans Vestberg (Ericsson), Jeff Immelt (GE), Ursula Burns (Xerox), Indra Nooyi (PepsiCo), and Bob Iger (Disney), among others—a total of 21 top-profile CEOs.

and your mind (contrary to your body) works best when it's cooler. Your body temperature starts dropping from around 6:30 to 7:00 P.M. and continues to do so until it hits the base at around 4:30 A.M. Then it starts rising again, signaling that it's time to wake up! It will take some time adjusting to the new schedule, but it will transform the way you work and produce many times the current results.

There are some mornings, however, when it's incredibly hard to concentrate or get going. You are up, but you don't want to start. At times like this, here's my advice: No action e-mails. No giving input to team members' work. No working on plans. At these dire moments, start by reading. Pick up a business book (or a self-help book—I am a junkie at this), and start reading your favorite passages. You will get the urge to work on the important stuff within 5 to 10 minutes.

PRINCIPLE 3 Catch Small Signals and Make a Difference

What are you good at? What are your strengths? I will give you a minute to write it down. I still remember a homework training exercise I did a while ago in which the facilitator told us to write down 100 different adjectives describing who we were on a piece of paper. It was a laborious effort—trust me, coming up with 100 positive words is not easy—but I did as instructed. In the end, she told us we had to circle a few words that resembled us most, then choose one final word out of those. Mine ended up being "interesting." I liked to do interesting things, meet interesting people, go to interesting places, and lead an interesting life. For example, I learned Chinese (my third language) over many years out of curiosity about what it would be like to master a new language. To my amazement, speaking Chinese now feels "innate"—that is, I have achieved critical inflection points and mastered native-level pronunciation. Isn't that interesting?

People who rise to leadership know more deeply who they are, what they are good at, and how to improve their strengths. But there is another, more subtle difference that I want to share with you. This technique sets leaders apart from others. At McKinsey, we focus on being *distinctive.* Throughout our consulting life, we are forced to think about this phrase after every project assessment (called the engagement performance review) and during our six-month review cycle (called the semi-annual review). A rating of *distinctive* is the highest rating you can get. When you are surrounded by people with outstanding skills, from top graduate programs, and who have a fast learning curve, it's really hard to show off or be *distinctive* by the traditional method of "working hard." It's safe to say that almost everyone in your crowd got here because they have worked extremely hard until now. So what else can you do?

You can catch small signals and make a huge difference. Does this sound familiar? Not surprisingly, it resembles the Pareto principle, or the 80-20 rule. The Pareto principle, discovered by economist Vilfredo Pareto, states that 20 percent of the input is responsible for 80 percent of the results. Pareto analysis is an efficient problem-solving technique. For example, on a failure analysis I once conducted, I found that 20 percent of the defective parts caused 80 percent of the engine malfunctions. But we always stop using the Pareto principle in the context of problem solving. We never take it one step further and apply it to our day-to-day life and our leadership careers. What if this thinking can significantly enhance your chances of success?

Once, an engagement manager told me that she helped her client prepare a speech in English. Being fluent in both Chinese and English, it was an easy task for her. She sat with the client and typed up in English what the client was saying in Chinese, in real time. The client, who was worried about becoming a train wreck in the presentation, thanked this engagement manager profusely. If the story just ended there, it wouldn't be so interesting. I forgot to add that this client was not even a core member of the client team. She was in a high position at the client company, but they'd only met once in a steering committee. What was amazing about this McKinsey colleague was that she happened to catch a small distress signal from the client that she needed help. So, willingly and without hesitation, she offered to help. Later, as the project moved forward, rumors spread that McKinsey really helps clients above and beyond the call of duty. With such a simple effort, she created a distinctive reputation both in the client's mind and among McKinsey leaders.

What I took away from this engagement manager's story is not just her ability to sense distress signals but her overall sensitivity to smaller signs. Once in Hong Kong, at the British healthy fast-food restaurant Pret A Manger, my colleagues were frantically debating the calorie consequences of getting a chocolate chip cookie on top of the sandwiches and salads they'd ordered. After they finished ordering *without* their cookies, they found out that the cashier had included *two* chocolate chip cookies with each meal, courtesy of the store! One of the astonished colleagues turned around and tried to pay, but the cashier just smiled and said, "Next time!" There's little doubt that those colleagues will again pay a visit to Pret A Manger when they go to Hong Kong, and maybe elsewhere. That cashier, as it turns out, also knew the trick of catching small signals.

So, what can you do beginning tomorrow, using your strengths, to make a huge difference from small things? I am *interested* to find out.

Principle 4 Have a 30-Second Answer to Everything

To impress someone fast, especially at the C level, short answers are important. Over the years, I've come to call it the 30-second answer to everything.

Being able to coherently and quickly put together loads of information, say from multiple interview sessions, is a rare ability. The synthesis can't be too detailed but also not too broad or high level. You also need to tailor the answer to your audience so that the hearers understand. Senior directors have a rare ability to tweak wavelengths, instantly. This ability takes practice, but it's something tangible that you can start doing today.

It starts by forming an answer beforehand. For example, recently, I had lunch with a former CEO of a sports manufacturing company. We were talking mostly about leadership development. Then he asked what else I was doing. I mentioned a recent lecturing opportunity I had. He asked on what topic. I told him that it was related to the organizational challenges faced in China. He asked, "So what are the organizational challenges?" This answer could get long, so I first gave him options. I listed the four different challenges with a quick sequential framework. He then zoomed in on the topic of "monetary compensation is not the biggest factor why employee retention is a problem." I had proposed that at the end of the sentence because I knew he would be interested in the topic of retention, training, and development.

Let's recap. It's not realistic to try to convey much meaningful information in a very short period of time. That's why you need to learn certain rules. The first rule is to understand the theory of "double-clicking." It's similar to when you read a comment or blurb of a certain product on an e-commerce site or a short summary snippet of a bestselling book. These tell you enough to get you interested but not nearly enough for you to know what's happening. So you end up clicking the link to find out more. In the same way, a 30-second answer gives your listener the opportunity to keep refocusing the attention to the topic of his or her interest.

Second, you need to get in the habit of taking apart the main question. Let's take another example. The C-level executive asks, "How is the project coming along?" Immediately you need to stand in the executive's shoes. What does he or she want to know? It's probably going to be along the lines of the four detailed questions below.

1. What is the overall project status, good or bad?
2. What are one or two examples that support the status?
3. What do I plan to do about any problems?
4. What can the C-level executive do to help?

Usually, the best way to think about the detailed questions is to put them through an algebraic framework. What key variables must be used in the equation to provide a meaningful output for the main question? As a general guideline, using some form of "stakeholder, process, and timeline" can help to structure the content.

Third, you need to constantly think of your answer like a dartboard. You are not starting from the innermost circle (the bull's-eye) but from the outermost ring. From the outermost ring you are trying to quickly hone into the center by giving the person easy-to-identify cues in your answers. Thus answering a question becomes more like an exercise of "preempting the question several steps beforehand," as if you were playing a game of chess and reading the opponent's potential moves. Below are several reasons why you should practice the 30-second answer:

1. You develop a keen sense of what people want.
2. You practice your synthesis skills.
3. You become a better presenter.
4. You subconsciously train your mind to reach the CEO level.

PRINCIPLE 5 Frontload Your Project

"The first day of any project needs to be as exhausting as the final day of the progress review," Diane, a former engagement manager

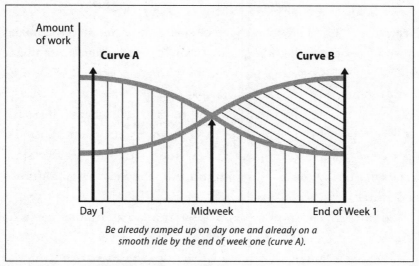

FIGURE 1.1: Frontloaded Versus Typical Work Curve

and now a professional development director, said to me during one session. You need to shine in the first week because that is when most of the impression about you will be decided by all of your stakeholders—your team, client, and senior leaders. Therefore, it is imperative that you bring in *as much as you physically and mentally can* during this period. It's a very vivid statement recalled by many other senior leaders during the interviews. What it boils down to is what McKinsey people call "preparing the one-week answer."

Take a look at Figure 1.1. This is the theoretical ramp-up of the curves A and B and their areas underneath the curve. Let's say the area under the curve is the output, or what's been completed. Curve A ramps up faster with the first day being the peak, while Curve B ramps up gradually, reaching its peak around the end of week one. This theoretical illustration shows the same amount of work completed (which equals the area under the curve) but very different implications. Clients and senior leaders will be much happier in case A than B.

Frontloading your project is a way to show how quickly you can learn your job, apply what you've learned, and take command of your lifestyle. A senior headhunter from Egon Zehnder, a prominent global executive search firm run by numerous former McKinsey consultants, told me that fast learners *and* doers have a high chance of landing executive management roles early because it's such a rare talent. In fact, because the current industry and business dynamic change so frequently, this is a highly sought-after skill. Thus mastering the essence of frontloading is a clear sign of future potential.

So how do you frontload your projects? What are the things to check?

There is a "basket of essentials" you need to prepare during the first week. Don't go into a project with a mindset that you plan to do "x" and "y" later. If you can do it now, just push and finish it.

1. Get senior leaders to spend as much time as possible with you. Ideally you will block at least a few hours of the senior leaders' time in the earlier days of the week. Ask assistants and make it happen. It is the mindset that's important. Before you may not have thought it was absolutely necessary to sit down very early in the game. Well, now you do. Two benefits arise from doing this: (A) You have a chance to possibly shape the outcome, project setup, and minor details beforehand. (B) You will be looked upon as a highly reliable and quick-to-ramp-up person with a fast learning curve.

2. Complete your end story line up front. The backbone of what makes McKinsey consultants powerful storytellers is that we are able to bring every fancy chart back to a few bullet points in a Word document. For example, when we did a growth and strategy project for a media conglomerate, we had only three guiding questions to answer. They were:

1. Where does the company stand today?
2. Where can the company compete, go tomorrow, and grow its business?
3. What kinds of capability building or resources are required?

As a leader, you want to avoid making people work on irrelevant tasks. You don't want to ask your team members to spend long hours making charts you end up not using. You lose credibility quickly that way. To avoid this, stick to your story line. Create a timeline. Then have a rough idea and work plan with a clear category breakdown for your team to plow through.

3. Get all your burning questions answered. Don't say, "I will ask that later." Contrary to our possible beliefs, asking is not a sign of ignorance or weakness. There are some tips to remember, however, so the delivery, timing, framing, and communication of the question do not make you sound incompetent. The general rule of thumb is to ask questions up front quickly before the week is over. This is the only "risk-free" asking period. McKinsey consultants learn this trick very early in their careers because after something has been said once, it will not be repeated. Second, use casual settings, such as coffee breaks, to ask sensitive questions such as a request to take a few days off on a busy week. It's easier to discuss frankly and off the record for both parties. (As an aside, an important thing to remember is to refrain from leaving any of these sensitive questions in writing, for example on e-mails, as many people will not be able to respond.) Third, try to reserve fact-based questions in the lower priority, unless it is urgent to know for the matter being discussed. Fact-based questions are seen as relatively easy questions to answer and can be done on your own time. (Refer to Principle 19: Pause Three Seconds Before Answering Difficult Questions for different categories of questions.) For example, if you are joining a project and want to know the details of proton therapy treatment, it is better to just grasp the one-line surface description and find out the details later—for example, by watching a YouTube video online that night. Lastly, develop a sense of priority in deciding which questions to ask. Here are examples of some pressing questions I keep in mind.

- Perspective-related questions: Who are the experienced stakeholders?
- Stakeholder and working engagement questions: What's the relationship challenge?
- Scope and end output goal alignment questions: What's the "best-case" scenario?
- Risk and constraint questions: What are the major pitfalls?

4. Do a quick due diligence on your team members. This comes in two aspects. First, call around people your team member has worked with and conduct a thorough check of his or her strengths and development before the project kicks off. Second, have a 30-minute, one-on-one talk with each individual on the first day not to discuss the project but to discover the learning and motivation for the individual. Most likely, the team member will have some idea about the project; you should set up a separate discussion regarding the scope, project responsibility, required tasks when you have mastered points 2 and 3.

5. Organize all necessary meetings. The first week should be spent locking in all necessary meetings. This may be truer for a consultant serving a client; nevertheless, securing the best dates for progress reviews and workshops is your topmost concern in projects. Like booking theater or concert tickets, the earlier you book, the better your seats. Also, at this point, when you do this logistic up front, you have an added benefit of realizing the key dates and expected resources you will need to pull together. For example, it may be the fastest way to realize that you only have 12 working days before the first progress review and you may need more time. It really puts your plans into perspective.

6. Delegate any work you don't need to handle yourself. Usually the following exercise on the first day works best. "Ask yourself, 'Between me and my bed, what prevents me from going to bed. What is the only thing I need to do before going to bed?'" says Diane.

Anything that is not really energizing you should be first confronted with a simple question, "Can someone else do this?" For example, buying certain things, fixing your Internet network, creating list of stakeholders' e-mail and telephone contacts, or paying for sundry expenses—list out all such tasks and ask whether you can delegate this work. Don't hesitate. You have plenty of other things to do during this first week. Focus all your attention on the core areas 1 through 5 as listed above.

Frontloading is a way to keep your head above the water. It is not only useful in the beginning of the project. The essence should stay with you throughout your career. If you are suddenly transferred to a new location to set up a branch office or appointed to construct the next distribution center in a new country, remember to push as much as possible during the first week. The trust, credibility, and confidence you will raise will be distinctive and unbeatable. Don't wait until later; get the chance to do it whenever possible.

PRINCIPLE 6 Create the Right End Output Image

The captain in the cockpit announces that your plane will land in 30 minutes. Uh-oh, you silently think to yourself. You still have 50 minutes left on your in-flight movie. What do you do? You most likely would quickly fast-forward the movie closer to the end. And just before electronic devices had to be turned off for landing, you would make a tight finish. Hurrah, you would smile. You got to watch the hero save another day.

Having an ending is important. It brings a sense of accomplishment and clarity. Without that you still feel something is unresolved.

For another example, let's say you hired McKinsey for some consulting work. Which of the following would you prefer to read as a client?

1. Twenty-five pages of fully completed deck with another 25 pages to come (the hypothetical title page specifies a 50-page deliverable)
2. Fifty pages of half-completed deck, with approximately 25 blank pages scattered throughout the document. But you see the first and last three pages are fully completed.

I hope you selected number 2. Of course, in a true context, the Firm will not deliver any unfinished output; but would it surprise you if I told you that internally, this level of completed document is already in circulation in the first week or so of a three-month project? In other words, McKinsey tries to put together an end-of-the-project output image as quickly as possible.

If you put these two obvious scenarios in a single frame, you emerge with a picture. It is important to present a case with the ending already factored in. People would rather skip over multiple scenes to finish the movie, and they'd definitely want to grasp the sense of how things will turn out for a business presentation. People don't like to wait. That is why you should learn to create an end output image all the time.

At McKinsey we call this end output image a dummy chart. Then we call the entire presentation material the ghost deck. All consultants share this common language to mean knowing what we want to complete. If the end output image is unclear we instantly raise the issue. Especially in consulting, where drawing out charts is a big chunk of our core job, testing senior leaders for a dummy or end output image reassures us that we are not concocting stuff out of thin air, or POOMA ("pulled out of mid air"). It eliminates a lot of waste and bogus work requirements for junior team members.

Thomas A. Edison was a legendary inventor with over 1,000 patents. When you picture this mastermind, there is a spitting image of "hard work, trial-and-error learning, and oomph" over talent. His famous saying, "Genius is 1 percent inspiration and 99 percent perspiration" is known to all, young and old. But what enabled him to pursue success with such great conviction was not just his sheer perseverance, effort, and luck but his power to envisage an end output. He already knew what a perfect and practical incandescent electrical lightbulb should look like. All he needed to do was to get there, through 10,000 times of failure.

Edison was a genius of the future. That was his strength. Let's say you are currently trying to start a business. You want to sell cookies. If someone from the future tells you with 99 percent conviction that your chocolate almond double-dipped cookie will become the next sensation, will you continue? Even in tough and demanding circumstances? Of course you will—you'll think you're sitting on a pot of gold. Work will not be work anymore. What made Edison an even greater end output visionary was that his vision did not just stop at the product level. It ended only when he saw many consumers using his lightbulbs: he had a product commercialization end vision. That was what made him different from the rest of the inventors. He fought hard for his patents. He knew that patents brought him extra money and monopoly.[3]

When you know what you want, you work better, faster, and more aggressively. Generally, people like to hear a top-down vision. To start top-down, you need to have prepared the end product—the answer—in advance rather than making it up as you go along. The speaker needs to know in advance, "I have three things I want to share with you: A, B, and C," instead of rambling from A to B to C and coming to a halt. The latter is uncertain; the former is definitive—and smart.

What is an end output image, exactly? Architects and designers use one all the time. It's a blueprint or backbone of something you are trying to create. Your goal is a work in progress, but we know how it'll turn out.

Hang Tight

In "hang tight" there are five principles to keep in mind.

PRINCIPLE 7

Smile When You Are Under Stress. During stressful meetings, keep on smiling to reduce your stress and stay focused on getting the work done.

PRINCIPLE 8

Go Beyond Your Self-Perceived Limit. Growth is not glamorous but painful, you need patience and action: reach out to think outside the box, and focus on the now.

PRINCIPLE 9

Always Imagine the Worst-Case Scenario. Imagining the worst-case scenario will enable you to make decisions more quickly and think about the next-step actions.

PRINCIPLE 10

Start Following Up. Following up is an important skill to boost your credibility and stay on top of your game; codify to-do items to make it possible.

PRINCIPLE 11

Push Back with Less Emotion. Use the 24-hour rule and an evaluation mechanism to push back logically; don't listen to anyone cruising at 33,000 feet!

PRINCIPLE 7 Smile When You Are Under Stress

Have you ever been in a situation where you were under a lot of stress? People in the meeting were determined to outright challenge your presence. All you could think about the entire time was how to get through it all—from the moment you walked in until you were done and told to leave. The entire process was not a pleasant one. But why should you make these happenings, which are to be expected in certain business situations, a negative experience?

Now, picture someone with a great big smile: your mentor, your boss, or a family member. What happens to you? Do you see yourself smiling a bit? When we see others in a positive state, we tend to emulate them. It's a natural reaction. Thus, smiling works especially well when you are in a situation where people least expect it. The higher up you go in the professional hierarchy, the better people are at hiding emotions underneath their smiles. It's an extraordinary skill, and few have recognized it as something extremely useful as a leader—till now.

Carmen, a senior engagement manager, is one such leader who was able to perform this smile early in her development. During our discussion, I could sense that her emotions remained extremely constant. She shared her story of how she learned to keep her composure and smile. She worked with a pharmaceutical client for six months as a fresh junior manager. The client boss was not happy most of the time and literally yelled and screamed during meetings. That was when one principal stepped in the way, always smiling under any fire. He didn't mind it at all.

How could he do it? And why does smiling have such a huge effect on people?

To understand the nature behind smiling in any situation, one must first learn to answer a few questions:

- What is the big picture?
- Are we trying to solve the same common issue just from different angles?
- Can I separate the problem from the person?
- What is the root cause of the hostility?

Usually, by having a different frame of mind, or trying to do so, one can cordially withdraw himself or herself from the current distress.

Understand that smiling reduces stress.[4] It creates positive emotions. When you smile, you tend to nod your head more, and the other person senses acknowledgment. This is usually returned by less anger. You, on the other hand, show more confidence.

Keeping a smile inevitably enables you to not lose your temper. You will think more logically and tend to be ahead of the other person, who might already be in a more complicated emotional state. This does not, however, mean to be indifferent or detached under the veil of a smile. You still have passion to agree or disagree, but by keeping a positive outward presence, you can keep the discussion going. Carmen told me her most notable incident with DHL, the German-based fast parcel delivery giant. DHL was supposed to deliver her passport from the agency that day but somehow got the logistic screwed up. Instead, the service told her to go pick up the documents in one of the DHL offices. She called the customer service agent to complain, but since she had a plane to catch that night she had no choice but to go the office—only to find that the passport had now been shipped back to her home! Fuming, Carmen chewed the customer service agent out on the phone. She said she's never been so angry at anyone. What she learned from, and later reflected, was how calm, helpful, and pleasant the agent was throughout the entire process. Of course, it was not the agent's fault. The logistics screwup happened on-site. But despite that, the agent listened to Carmen's clamoring with positive silence. So, in the end, Carmen decided to let it go.

One word of caution is that smiling can sometimes provoke the other person to become even angrier. You need to practice your smile so that in such a situation it is decently favorable and not an inappropriate, over-the-top gleaming smile. Of course, people in the discussion know you can't be truly happy and that your smile is purposeful. Nevertheless, the effort to keep things in control, for you and for your counterpart, is what counts. It's much better than having a stern, negative, or even dismissive facial expression.

Keep smiling!

PRINCIPLE 8 Go Beyond Your Self-Perceived Limit

A mentor and friend said to me long ago, "A strong will is an unspoken art."

Sometimes you encounter unbelievably tough circumstances. You are lost. You are beat. You are desperate. The situation is so overwhelming that you are in a state of paralysis, both mentally and physically. Throwing in the towel right about now seems like the only option. You can't possibly go on like this to the final round.

Tina is one of the toughest, most unwavering project leaders at the Firm. She leads young analyst trainings with a voice that booms across the entire floor. For her, being distinctive is about being confident and having faith.

Tina had a very tough pharmaceutical client one year whom the Firm hadn't served for a long time. The client stretched the project scope, and the Firm sent in a "1 + 5" team (one engagement manager and five business analysts or associates). Tina was the manager on the project. Halfway through the 15-week study, the situation became so unbearable that Tina was about to send an e-mail to the principals telling them "I will not be coming in anymore." According to Tina, each work stream on this project was equivalent to an entire project compared to other projects she had handled before. But despite her all-in efforts, the clients were unhappy, the team was exhausted, and even the senior leaders were overstretched, which exacerbated her self-doubt. Two senior leaders were supportive, but that just made things worse for her. Thoughts such as "Even with their support, I may not be able to pull a decent job off," haunted her day and night.

At critical breakdown point such as this, *How should one hang in there?* Let's reflect upon a few important takeaways.

First, when you are stretched you need to acknowledge this. Let it sink in. Pause. Then tell yourself, "There is no such thing as glamorous growth but only painful growth. The glamor comes only in hindsight." In desperate times, the pressure and stress will force you to become pessimistic and shortsighted. Understand at this phase that you may feel like you are not growing and are lost.

Second, you need to be aware that developing a new capacity to handle things requires patience *and* action. Tina's mind needed to be told time and again, "I don't know how to do it today, but I will know how to do it tomorrow and do it." You need to move forward. Take incremental steps. The worst thing is to complain and do nothing. Rather than blaming or whining, what one must do is to acknowledge that "everyone will experience the bottom of the ocean, but we will definitely swim back up." One of the many things I have learned from my wife, also a McKinsey consultant, is that she never complains. She always says, "If you are going to complain, blame, or criticize, then do something about it." Dale Carnegie, the pioneer of self-improvement professional training, said, "Feeling sorry for yourself, and your present condition, is not only a waste of energy but the worst habit you could possibly have."

Third, reach out. Share your pain points with others. If you hold it in, you will dive into a negative spiral. "In extremely tortuous nights, I would even call my mentor after midnight because I couldn't focus on the deliverables," Tina recalls, shaking her head. She said she continued to work her way forward until her stress leveled off. Her mentor told her that usually in situations like this the problem is not only "you" but other complications you don't see. It's true. When there are a dozen things shaping the situation, we tend to blame everything on the wrong things. Thus, it is important to have a genuine and caring advisor to give you the right perspective. Reaching out will allow you to think outside the box.

Fourth, you have to stop thinking about past failures and future uncertainties. Daniel Millman, author of the book *Way of the Peaceful Warrior*, says that we each have two major "mind" channels: one is the mind that thinks in the past or the future, and the other is the mind that lives the now. To control the two settings, all it takes is for you to become aware of which mode you are in. If there is a small demon that appears during tough circumstances, it will definitely try to snatch you into the past or future mode. You need to lock him up. Successful leaders always turn to the next problem and the next solution. More than ever, in a tough situation, go into the "ticking the checkbox" mode.

After going through this monumental study, Tina says she is not afraid of climbing into tough situations. "This week, I joined my third project for a client. It was already midway into it and I had a lot of catching up to do, but I found there was substantial reward. I truly felt the benefit for hanging in there," she said with an upbeat tempo.

Show your vulnerability, but have faith. You will succeed. Growth is not glamorous.

PRINCIPLE 9 Always Imagine the Worst-Case Scenario

The fear of failure is always demotivating. But most times, the worst thing is really not that bad. To help you keep going, learn to overcome the fear of failure by imagining the worst.

Have you ever wondered why some people are calm in high-stress situations? Or, why some are able to make decisions quickly when things go wrong? Strong leaders, especially at the Firm, have a knack for making things go well when all goes to hell. During interviews for the right candidates to join the Firm, we look for success-hungry individuals who are more adventurous and willing to go out of their way to get things done.

Consultants always need to be asking, "Can we do even better? What else are we missing?" types of questions. Over the years of apprenticeship at the Firm, many are groomed to think about two major aspects of the job:

1. Visualizing and ghosting out the ideal end output of the project, which later transforms into foreseeing higher strategic missions for clients
2. Having a ready-made countermeasure in place or prearranged team problem-solving meetings when something flares up

We do this because it achieves two great mindsets. The first one allows us to see what an ideal best-case scenario may look like and pushes our thinking to the next level. Senior directors and principals push the envelope to help us see a better, even crisper ideal state. The second one allows us to see what we can do right away when a bad-case scenario hits home. Thus, in other words, this simple exercise allows you to develop the mind to see both ideal and nonideal situations.

Many organizations and people working on different projects are prone to hiccups—you can't avoid pitfalls and mistakes. The difference between a great team leader and a mediocre one when it comes to facing such situations is whether the leader goes into "firefighting" mode or has a "countermeasure-driven" action plan. The former is not really a mindset; such leaders are, like firefighters, extinguishing fire when alerted. Sometimes they are successful and other times not. They lack the necessary mental preparation and appropriate countermeasures. During my career, I have witnessed several people who have thought only about "when it goes right" but not "what if it goes wrong."

Truth be told, I was a notorious example at that. Because I wanted things to go perfectly, every Sunday at dusk, I would sit down to review my project progress underneath a weight of "how to make things right." Luckily, for a few projects that worked. When I crash-landed in one of my other projects, I learned that those Sundays should be spent thinking not only about the best outcome but also about the worst outcome. To take your thinking a step further, consideration of the worst outcome should be supplemented with knowing whom to talk to and what concrete steps are going to be effective. Coming back to the question asked earlier in this section, leaders who stay calm in times of stress or who are able to make decisions quickly when problems arise can do so through years of practicing this trained art.

Where do we see an example of creating such scenarios in business cases? Take, for example, a strategic project or due diligence in merger and acquisition work. Here you will often come across multiple scenarios. You create different versions of the external reality—the macro environment and competitors. As well, you dive into internal changes—company growth and/or decay. These are usually categorized in three buckets called base, best, and worst-case scenarios. Investors are interested in knowing how a company would fare even at its worst case. Therefore, in your day-to-day work, you should also care about how to do well when things are bad.

In a project work setting, defining your worst case scenario has a few obvious benefits.

> First, you control your emotions better, hence allowing a healthy state of mind. Your top anxieties fall as you participate in the anticipation. When something bad does happen—for example, your progress review didn't go as well as expected—you have made plans for your next move and move on.
>
> Second, it allows you to cover more ground. Let's say the worst-case scenario is that your supporters for promotion all abandon you. As a precautionary measure, then, you may try to get an additional two or three other supporters from another subset of people. You may decide to hold more touch points with these individuals. You will come up with a more foolproof mechanism, and you will be positive that you have done your best.

Over the years, in getting better at predicting worst-case outcomes, I picked up poker games as a social activity. Playing games like Texas Hold'em teaches you a few valuable lessons. The most important lesson is how to play not to lose. The second lesson is to set a cap or maximum loss. The third is keeping calm when you have a bad losing streak. Keeping a poker face is not only about hiding your emotions about the cards you have but also about hiding your emotions in entirety throughout all matches. The fourth is to imagine the worst night possible. For me, that would be to get cleaned out in less than 15 minutes. The common theme in all four lessons is deliberation on downside risk and not upside reward. If you go into the game thinking you will win big—the best-case scenario—and end up losing big, you feel terrible. If you go into the game thinking you may lose big—the worst-case scenario—and end up doing a lot better, you feel great.

Setting your worst-case scenario expectation is best done at the beginning of the project and right before the final or important milestone. The beginning is crucial for you to set your expectation and be mentally ready for any bad outcome. The timing before the final or important milestone is to focus on risk mitigation as much as possible.

PRINCIPLE 10 Start Following Up

On one occasion, my colleague saw a young consultant under scrutiny for not remembering past discussions. "That point, if you remember, we discussed it three months ago!" or "Why are you bringing up something already closed weeks ago!" and so on. The director was irked. The consultant was now frantically flipping through pages and taking notes. But it was to no avail: the director had lost all confidence in him.

Following up is an art. The mastery does not come overnight. It's important, everyone knows it. But it's difficult to put it in practice. Why is following up important? That's easy: it's because you don't want to miss any important opportunities and want to avoid major losses. It's also important because you want to show presence, awareness, and a solid reputation. It's a way to reach higher maturity and build stronger credibility fast. Being able to follow up is not only very important for the obvious roles such as in a sales-oriented function (for example, being able to recall past conversations accurately) but also for administrative functions such as HR. It is a universally recognized, clearly intuitive, and extremely coveted skill, yet you have probably only seen a handful of people grasp it well.

Why is that?

1. Following up is perceived as a minor theme. Unlike updating or completing to-dos, following up is a low-profile action. Unless you decide to do this, no one will really push you to become an expert at it. Of course, you may get reprimanded by your client or your senior leader for forgetting something, but it usually ends up as a "one-time" thing, and when it's over, you don't come back to "follow up on your missed follow-up." Therefore, when the meeting is over, and your firefighting is done, you feel at peace with the task itself rather than diving down to the root cause of why it happened.

2. Rereading notes, unless you have made it a habit, is cumbersome. We all have busy lives. For some reason, we tend to go back to our notes only when we need to—mostly when someone asks for something or when we need to write up something. Then you no doubt start reading more of your notes. You can put rules like, "At the end of my day I will spend 10 minutes to go back through my notes," but it rarely works. People are driven mostly by a sense of urgency.

3. Overreliance and confidence in memory. We consultants have an old saying, "It is better to take notes and free your mind for problem solving," and so should you. Our mind and memory are really not so reliable. Recovered memory, for example in eyewitness testimony in court, has always been controversial because our memory tends to distort reality due to stress, passage of time, and external influences.[5]

As a prerequisite, good follow-up requires codification. Diane, quoted earlier in the frontloading principle, says, "The note-taking skill is the prerequisite to become good at following up. Use simple codes. Circles, squares, and highlighters help. It needs to be quickly replicable and complete." She is known by internal colleagues and external clients as a follow-up master. Clients have copied her note-taking style. For example, in an innovation workshop, Diane first places squares for all the necessary to-dos. Then she uses a yellow highlighter to highlight points she knows will last several weeks. For longer items that will take a few months for completion, she uses a different color. If the follow-up has been closed, she will use an orange highlighter to show it's done. She does not cross out items but keeps them for a record.

You can also give yourself some other minor rules to enable better follow-up. For example, one principal said that after he finishes an expert interview call or deep discussions with clients, he always sends back his key learning, summarized neatly into three or four core themes. It helps him remember particular details effectively. Another director said it is important not to feel uncomfortable to ask clients out on meals even after the project is finished. This is also a form of follow-up he constantly advises to budding leaders. You don't need a specific reason or a purpose, your goal is to just "follow up."

Lastly, if I think I may have even the slightest chance to forget something (it happens quite often), I make sure I capture it right away on a paper napkin or the back of a receipt. Until you get yourself that assistant who beeps you for every single detail and person to meet, learn to make following up a habit.

PRINCIPLE 11 Push Back with Less Emotion

Some people are great at pushing back and others are not. What is the difference?

THE 24-HOUR RULE

Logical thinking requires your emotions to stay calm. But when we are asked to do overwhelming tasks, our instinctive reaction kicks in where emotion takes over logic. Usually these negative feelings take a lot more time to subside than you would think. Dave, a senior principal, told me one of the best pieces of advice he received from his mentor was thinking out the "24-hour rule." Every time at work someone gives you something outrageous to do, wait for 24 hours before you act upon it with a counteroffer. There are two basic underpinnings for this rule:

1. People (and usually senior leaders) have the best interests of you and the company at heart.
2. You will tend to regret any negative or rebuking answers you make when you are under emotional siege.

For instance, say there is a senior director who always forces you to prepare presentation decks before any client proposal, big or small. For some, when the issue is relatively clear, you agree that preparing a hypothesized presentation on the problem will greatly increase your chances of bidding the project. On others, the information is still quite gray and useless. The tricky part is always this: you are never sure on the spot of such prediscussions, and your judgment is clouded by your eagerness not to waste valuable time. You would like to focus on what matters most. Under these circumstances, give each situation a 24-hour check-in period. This way, you have more dictating power over them. Try the 24-hour rule when you get the urge to push back with emotions or you are not 100 percent sure. At least by following such a rule you will be more convinced with your work when you have to give it all in, and you will come out with a more serious and committed outcome, a win-win.

Usually when you are assigned to a new task, you tend to start worrying right away about *how* to do it—the resources, time, and capability. It's because you are conditioned to think this way. Instead, first try to take a step back and ask yourself a simple question: "*What* is the objective, or *why* are we doing this?"

A client once requested a colleague of mine to convert a 100-page PDF file into PowerPoint slides. The client stressed its importance and urgency, but instead of getting right to work, my colleague, who is adept at pushing back, skillfully found out that what the client wanted was just to combine the two files for easier distribution. So my colleague suggested creating a point in the agenda section to refer to the PDF file instead. This neatly solved the problem in five minutes rather than two days of painful hard work. At McKinsey, although this type of work can usually be outsourced to our production team, it is still imperative to have a good practice at heart.

Second, assess the value of your efforts by quickly doing a back-of-the-envelope calculation to see if the impact is big enough. This will help you drill down into the *why* question with more precision. It should be a number-driven effort, if possible. Both figuring out the objective and estimating an impact number should give both parties a clear idea of the task's relative significance. For example, I had a lighting client once who wanted us to jointly develop an end-to-end transformation plan for automotive lights and air purifiers. My client counterpart was a smart, practical, and quick-on-his-toes kind of guy who was able to consistently bring the discussion back to core numbers. After our initial diagnosis across three different markets, we found that (A) the redefined market size was much smaller than the client's previous estimates, and (B) the market showed only a low single-digit growth. While other department heads were pushing for more resources to conduct right channeling, partnerships, and customers, he pushed back. He knew the objective: transformation. He knew the compelling numbers. Even if the department heads wanted more resources to fix the problem, the problem was not there. He asked, shouldn't we revisit our entire strategy? I couldn't have agreed more. I knew it wasn't the ideal answer for McKinsey, but it was the best decision for him and the

	What is the objective?	Is the impact big enough?	Are we the right people to do it?	What's the timeline?
Deeper level	✓ Step back from your role as a project leader and ask, does it make sense objectively?	✓ Evaluate actual value, perceived value, and the time and effort the task will take.	✓ Make sure that this team and its members are the best fit to carry out the role.	✓ Timing can usually be adjusted, and very urgent tasks are limited.
Tone	Open dialogue and in the other person's shoes	Number-driven, less emotional	Collaborative and want to maximize output	Neutral but care about the final deadline
Decision	Go or no go	Go or no go	Go, resource optimization	Go, sensible date decision

FIGURE 1.2: Evaluation Process for Pushing Back

client. I was right alongside him to acknowledge the merit of his suggestion, and the exploration team was dissolved.

Only when both objective and impact are relevant, then you move on to the required people, capability, and timeline validation—the *how* effort. Figure 1.2 shows a quick evaluation process I use. You start with the objective, then measure the impact, and follow it up with a question of personnel fit and the required level of urgency. This process will assert more control over the project and a sense of reliability for you as a leader.

CRUISING AT AN ALTITUDE OF 33,000 FEET

Senior leaders—in McKinsey's case, directors—love to contribute ideas to your project; many of them are great ideas indeed. But you need to understand that these leaders have many other projects running at the same time. Unless the person is the direct boss or client counterpart, "As a general rule of thumb," a principal once said to me, "try to ignore the majority of inputs by saying something like, 'I like these three ideas (out of the 10), and I want you to take me deeper into those,' and refocus only on those great ideas, not on the seven others you want to drop. It works on *selective memory* effort. Usually, the other seven will be forgotten." If it happens that the person keeps coming back at point number four or nine, then you know it is really important. But what if the senior director adamantly wants to keep all 10? Adopt the hypothesis that he has good intentions and try to understand *why* he might be saying that. At this point it is important to determine whether that person is too far off and just wants to implement whatever best practice efforts he's seen in the past—which we call cruising at 33,000 feet—or if he or she is helping you solve your specific problems. You will be able to come to good terms with the person as long as you stay on the positive perception.

This thinking seems to be shared across the Firm. According to Jeongmin, an associate principal with a reputation of being a trusted turnaround man, "Great project leaders receive 10 inputs and make that into 5 on the spot. Mediocre ones take all 10. The worst ones make it into 20. It is always better to deliver on three and produce a 120 percent output rather than deliver on 10 and produce a 60 percent output."

Above all, remember that people who are great at pushing back get a lot of work done, formulate their own approach such as the 24-hour rule or an evaluation process, focus on the positive side of things, and respond less emotionally.

Multiple Reflections

In "multiple reflections" there are five principles.

PRINCIPLE 12
Be Flexible on the Perception of Your Passion. Develop some form of passion in your current work so that you get fired up.

PRINCIPLE 13
What Would Marvin Do? Find Your Role Models. Identify different role models to fit your development goals—the more the merrier.

PRINCIPLE 14
Know What Gives You the Most Energy in Your Day. Manage your energy gains and drains via knowing what you like and dislike throughout the day.

PRINCIPLE 15
Go Jogging to Smell the Flowers. Help prolong your perceived time and set priorities through detaching yourself from daily preoccupations.

PRINCIPLE 16
Create a Commitment Plan. Achieve greater things in life by setting aspirational targets and sticking through your plan.

PRINCIPLE 12 Be Flexible on the Perception of Your Passion

Read the three sentences below and tell me which one sounds like an honest expression of someone with passion. Then rank them in the order of most to least credible.

I have a passion for . . .
1. Helping people solve problems
2. Improving the healthcare system
3. Baking cakes and opening a patisserie

Let me guess. Did you pick number 3 as most honest? And did you order the sentences 3, 2, 1? Why? Well, that's because the third sentence is more concrete and tangible than the second one and the second one more so than the first. I once believed passion is something that appears in a magic crystal ball. It's deep and profound. It's exciting to hear. It's unique and different. But I have altered this perception.

It didn't occur to me until much later in my leadership journey that passion has many different layers. It is not confined to only one definition. Nor does it have to be very specific for it to make sense or hold a rightful place in our hearts. Instead, it can come in all sorts of sizes and shapes. It just needs to speak for you.

Getting back to the three examples above, apparently all three are correct in terms of portraying the honesty of an individual's passion. A senior director at the Firm told me his passion was genuinely solving problems. Although he served a few big pharmaceutical clients, his drive to get up every morning and enjoy working was in the innate problem-solving process. The more obscure and perplexing his clients' situations got, the more fired up he became. He loved going into the complicated maze and finding his way out again. You could tell he wasn't making this up. His enthusiasm was strong, already counting 17-plus years at the Firm.

Tim was a medical doctor before he joined the Firm—a little less than five years ago. Now, he is a principal. After a few years at McKinsey he decided he wanted to build out a healthcare practice for McKinsey in Australia because it was virtually nonexistent. He flew to London on a mission, stayed for a year, and came back with the know-how and a bucketful of eager supporters. His eyes illuminate when you talk to him about his passion: "My intent was genuine because I was so excited about the topic. In most cases, finding your passion is always a battle between the *opportunities you can have* and what you are *essentially good at*. So I add a third element and ask, what *excites me most?*"

The third example is a former business analyst who turned into a pâtissier and now operates his own cake store. All three of them are legitimate and are real cases of passion. All three people get excited when they talk about their passion; it's what drives them to get up and energized about work every morning.

Therefore it's important to find your own form of passion. You don't need it to match with someone else's. As long as you know that that is what gets you fired up, you stick to it and keep working hard at it. I believe too many people waste precious time molding and scaffolding their passion to fit the right medium. For instance, they adamantly need to differentiate their passions from what they currently do, being unsatisfied with their job. Yet, passion can be as rudimentary as developing people, immersing in multiple projects simultaneously and becoming ignited by the sense of busyness, seeing things change dramatically, or building a series of sub-businesses.

Some people also incorrectly equate passion with the level of expertise on a subject. For example, don't think that you can't really have a passion for problem solving because people in many different fields are also adept at problem solving. Really, it doesn't matter if you are a business guru or a college student. There are no minimum requirements that must be reached to convince you or others.

Passion can be a combination as well. You can be passionate about developing people, problem solving, and healthcare. It doesn't need to be single-sided. As you can have passion doing many different things at once, you can also have multiple passions.

Then there is the link effort. Let's say you are passionate about leadership development. But you decided to join the Firm and your first project is in the mining sector doing resizing—seemingly irrelevant to what your passion is about. Many people may stop there. They will just wait for the next opportunity to join a study linked to their passion. However, a more proactive approach—taking your fate in your own hands—is to aggressively find a link within the project. You can definitely propose leadership development opportunities for the client managers. It's very normal during our day-to-day work that we don't get our foot in the right door. The key is to keep high hopes, be positive minded, and find your own bridge.

Passion can be accidental—but only on the surface. A lot of entrepreneurs claim their idea came to them accidently, such as one individual who started renting out airbeds to cover rent (Brian Chesky, Airbnb), or another trying to solve a vacuum cleaner clogging problem (Sir James Dyson, Dyson), or one lucky man who found his calling when swimming with the dolphins in Hawaii (Marc Benioff, Salesforce.com). These "accidental ideas" came to them because they each had an underlying passion. Chesky, with a failed cereal business, still passionately wanted to start up something. Sir Dyson had his flaming torch for inventions. Benioff, who took a sabbatical from Oracle, sought to provide a spiritual goodness in business and technology.[6]

There is no guiding principle of passion. It's what you choose to believe. What's important is finding the energy that makes you happy and fired up in the morning. Throughout my life, I've always admired people who could get up in the morning and get excited to go to work. I had to force myself at first. I created a bunch of external triggers in the morning—taking a shower, going walking, and drinking coffee—to set me in motion. But these people just naturally do, do, do. They don't stop. They are constantly in the now. It's awe-inspiring. It also made me wonder why. Where does it come from? Are they just born to such discipline? Or is it out of necessity? Then I met someone, my wife, whose passion (at least one of them) is in *doing* things. She just can't stay put, she needs to be productive every day. She gets up very early in the morning *every day, including Saturdays and holidays,* and does something.

So there you go. Elon Musk, the serial entrepreneur and Oracle inventor who founded SpaceX and cofounded PayPal and Tesla said, "Boil things down to the fundamental truths and reason up from there." His passion probably lies in the elemental, the periodic table of thought and building new things. That's why he can traverse across industries in multiple dimensions.

Try to grab onto anything you do that sparks your inner something—whatever diamond in the rough it may be—and walk out with it. The important message here is that you want to be fired up and investing 120 percent of your energy in something whenever possible. Thus, be flexible in your perception of passion. It will enable you to excel and grow faster.

PRINCIPLE 13 "What Would Marvin Do?" Find Your Role Models

Sometime during your career, you will be faced with making sensitive decisions. When you take the leap to leadership roles, presumably, you have already dealt with this issue or will deal with it soon. It's an inevitable path, and you need to be equipped with the right mindset.

McKinsey consultants have a saying, "What would Marvin do?" Marvin refers to the Firm's founding managing director, the late Marvin Bower (1903–2003), who shaped the Firm's values and the way modern management consulting is practiced today. Marvin was a strong advocate of having role models. The question is raised when consultants believe the work does not bring about positive change or impact for the client, or when certain actions go against the greater good of the society but benefit the sole entity. During an individual's McKinsey career, it is not rare to see client engagements get terminated or turned down based on these principles and impact limitations. A famous story known to all consultants is how Marvin turned away billionaire industrialist and aviator Howard Hughes on the basis that his management style and organization didn't want to be managed. I still remember one of my interviews when a senior principal told me the benefit of working in McKinsey is that you learn to avoid doing the *wrong* things. Thus, terms such as "obligation to dissent," which means to speak up to seniors when you think something is wrong, is not just a paper metaphor but is used regularly by consultants of various tenures.

This way of having integrity and sound judgment taught at the Firm is the ethos to successful leadership. Consultants learn that professional conduct is imperative to succeed at the Firm and also when they go on to do other profound endeavors. From the start, consultants learn not to disclose confidential material or names to third parties, including friends. I have yet to meet any Firm consultant who has given a client name away to external people, even among close friends, when working for the Firm (and many after they leave). Why? What drives someone to be so dedicated to the code? Enforcing good conduct is not easy, especially when it's something as informal as a name of a client. The first casual conversation you strike when you engage a friend at a dinner table is, "So what are you up to recently?" Then following your ambiguous answer of project topic and industry, your friend says, "So, are you helping Pfizer, or Johnson and Johnson?" At that point, it's so easy to just nod. But consultants don't. Why?

This is where the question "What would X do?" or having a role model becomes the key. Many consultants look up to the parental figure or role model from whom we have learned our trade. Because the Firm is closer to the "mastery of the art" philosophy, consultants are not bounded by fear of punishment for breaking the code, but rather by setting a good example. One time, I overheard a senior associate who was in a rush to get a PowerPoint document sent to her inbox. On the phone the other colleague nerve-rackingly said to her, "Let me try Gmail to send it over because the global VPN (virtual private network) is down." Given the time pressure, it sounded all right, but it breached the security conduct. The senior principal wanted to see the file within the hour. But instead, the senior consultant responded, "I will go over and get the file in person. Or can you deliver it? Meanwhile I will write an e-mail to change our discussion time with the principal." I am not sure what happened after that, but it exemplified a very good code of both setting a good example and doing it the right way.

Having a role model in mind does not just stop at dealing with sensitive topics. It has a positive influence on a range of things including dealing with your team, dealing with your client, and talking to your superiors. It is especially useful in communication and decision making. For example, when writing an e-mail to superiors to ask for permission, it usually works best to keep it short but convincing. When looking over the words, don't just step back and use a third-person view; instead, reread it as if you were the senior leader whom you admire. How would he write the letter to me? What words would he choose? Would he be more subtle or more direct? Then take one more step back and ask, "Wait, should I even write an e-mail? Or just ask him on the phone or outside the office?" Now you have stepped into the recipient's MO (modus operandi), which is by far the most effective way of engagement. By using a role model, you just went from "Am I writing the correct content on the e-mail?" to "Should I even write an e-mail?"

Human beings have a tendency to frame things in a narrow way. A role model lets you take away that narrow frame and see the big picture. Try to create role models for different occasions and not a "few fit all" model. For instance, I love playing tennis. When you are playing tennis, you most likely will not have any of your colleagues or seniors as your role model; instead it's your coach, your high school rival, or, maybe Roger Federer. But what's less obvious is assigning specific role models for different shots: backhand like your high school rival, volley like the coach, and game planning like Roger Federer (if you can!). In a business context, you can do the same. Go into the granularity of, say, presentations: for small meetings I will act like person A and for big meetings like person B. They are two different skills. You should have at least a dozen people in your role model Hall of Fame.

PRINCIPLE 14 Know What Gives You the Most Energy in Your Day

Your workload can be vastly different on any given day. You can expect some days to be much more stressful and busy. On these days, you are typically not in control of your schedule, completing tasks left and right and running to many meetings back-to-back. You have let "the fate of the day" control you and have drained your energy out completely. If you think about it for a second, what usually drains most of your physical and mental energy comes from stress due to this lack of control. A single philosophy separates successful leaders-to-be and the lackluster: all leaders know how to get energy from their time and release stress out of their systems.

Almost half a decade ago, I was watching a documentary on Ichiro Suzuki, a Hall-of-Fame bound Japanese baseball player who has played for the New York Yankees and Seattle Mariners, assessing the reasons behind his outstanding hitting records. About midway through the documentary, the interviewer asked him what he did on a regular basis to combat stress and fatigue. Ichiro responded (paraphrased), "The stress you get in baseball can only be 'paid back' in baseball. Therefore, to relieve my stress I don't do 'other' things. When I have a bad hitting day, I know the only way to get the bad feeling out of the system is to, well, practice. So I go at it." When I heard that, I quickly realized that successful people have a tuned-in mindset not only on how they achieve outstanding goals but also in their approach to dealing with the stress and energy drain that everyone faces.

In a regular work context, we are not up against reaching high batting averages. It's a bit grayer. Therefore, when you are busy, you need to know what will be important for you to get your energy back and reduce your stress levels. For example, if talking to people gives you special energy, make sure you don't end up staying in one room all day preparing your PowerPoint presentation or creating an Excel model. Likewise, if you know a few quiet hours a day will put you or your team back on track, you take it. At the same time, there are things that consume your energy. For example, for me, frequent small updates, making lists, running errands, scheduling, and logistics drain energy. Therefore, it is not a wise idea for me to put all these administrative tasks on one particular day, as I will not have a chance to get my energy back. In other words, you need to come up with a simple list of things you know you like and will give you back energy and things you know you dislike that consume your energy and hence will increase your stress. Knowing what gives you energy is a way to keep your mental health in check. A general rule of thumb is to remember the 7–3 rule. During the week, count how many "positive energy" things stack up against "negative drains" and make sure you have a healthy 7–3 ratio.

Then, as a forward-looking exercise for the following week, look at your current schedule and figure out if the positive-energy activities will give you the necessary counterbalance. Much of this may sound intuitive. The key point here is to adopt an energy-giving mode. Treat your mental health the way you treat your body.

Somehow, a lot of us are misjudged by a busyness index in our present work world—how much of our day is covered in colorful meetings. One of the most effective ways to get your energy back and take stress off at work is to block chunks of time out for yourself. You can block out half a day or a whole day, for example, to dedicate time for reflection. You can use that time to fix the most urgent problem at hand or to concentrate on your learning goals. Tim, a principal passionate about healthcare, told me he blocks out Wednesdays. Knowing that he has this time on his calendar allows him to stop worrying he won't have enough time to focus on important tasks. I asked him how that pans out in terms of others' expectations. He said, "It's not about can I, but just doing it, as you get so many more pluses than minuses from blocking time out." What helps, he advises, is using a simple rule of "delete, delegate, de-spec, and defer" many tasks so you can open up your day. The term de-spec means to reduce a certain task complexity into immediate next steps. So, for example, instead of writing, "Plan for next month's conference," you may want to just write, "Meet with counterpart on creating an agenda."

Finally, an important thing to remember is that successful leaders *leave* their problems and stress at work. You should learn to do that as well. Many people believe that the biggest antidote to immediate stress at work is going away on vacation or distancing yourself from the problem. Although this does help you get a bird's-eye-view on your problems, it will never be a long-term solution. Realize this and commit to pursuing real activities you know will help you directly reduce stress and fatigue at work.

PRINCIPLE 15 Go Jogging to Smell the Flowers

In one of my favorite movies about life's extraordinary gift, *Dead Poets Society*, English teacher John Keating (played by the late Robin Williams) tells his elite prep school students to "Carpe diem," Latin for "Seize the day." For me this fits perfectly in today's high-paced work environment.

Time is precious. In doing a simple, short, and measured exercise routine, there is a huge payout on actual time spent versus perceived time gains. In other words, some exercises allow you to stretch or prolong the time you feel and smell the outside world. It's such a rare and important feeling that you crave when you are working in an intense environment. For me, running fits this mode perfectly due to its extremely hassle-free setup: you can run virtually anywhere with just your running shoes.

When you run for 30 minutes, for example, your perceived time slows down. In a busy day, a whole afternoon can go by in a flash. You need a way to control your psychological time, especially to distance yourself from normal distractions and preoccupations. Oftentimes, when you are busy caught up in your work you miss out on prioritizing other important things in your life such as relationships, health, and big-picture goals. Jogging and other forms of "alone-time" exercise allow you to structure your thoughts clearly and set your top priorities straight. Scientists now say that during the day we should get up and move about. It stimulates our brain with better blood circulation and more oxygen. But that's not the only benefit. When we engage in an even longer exercise like jogging, our brain gets to take a rest from its default mode or inward-focused state—known as *self-referencing* in neuroscience—and be more attuned to the outer environment.[7] By shifting in and out of these two states of mind—reference to ourselves versus our environment—we get a new frame of reference to our lives that empowers us to look at things in a different light. Sometimes

McKinsey people like to call a similar phenomenon "stepping back" to see the bigger picture. But that is a mental exercise. This is an actual physical exercise that allows the brain to physically switch modes. Therefore, this type of exercise enables you to get a better and healthier lifestyle.

So how do you put this into practice?

1. Run during the day or at night. Many people go running in the morning. You have more control over time. You feel refreshed afterward. There are plenty of great reasons. Yet, physically speaking, running during the day or at night is better than morning. The science is because your body temperature is warmer, your reflexes are better, and your joints are more flexible at these times. Thus, you are less likely to get injured. Others like to go running at noon because it is the warmest time of the day throughout the seasons. For "summarizing your day" purposes, however, I've found night a far more effective "tool." Usually, most people can get some time off from work either during or after the dinner hour. When you do so, you may suddenly have an aha moment or see everything come together from the day's turmoil because you were able to distance yourself. Remember also, the mornings should be used to work on the hard stuff. So if you do like running in the morning, make sure you limit it to less than half an hour.

2. Run for time rather than distance. This is really up to the individual, but time works better than distance. You are not competing, thus the habit is more important than the achievement in terms of distance. Usually, running for around half an hour works best because you are well exercised but not exhausted.

3. Create a goal. It is easier to run regularly if you have a goal. I chose to run a half marathon five months after I started running regularly with a friend. Most readers of this book, guessing you are all high-achievers, probably yearn for growth and progress. Therefore, a half marathon is a good target to start with. Afterward, you could frame a nice picture and a medal for finishing from the Shanghai International Marathon or the Boston Marathon—a definite ego booster! Then you can move on to the next stage: Olympic triathlon, like my friend does, or if you are up for the challenge, a half Ironman.

4. Run alone. On the weekend, you can run, swim, play basketball, play tennis, or practice badminton with as many people as you want. But on this particular exercise to slow your mind, you have to do it alone. Usually a treadmill in the gym is most convenient. When you get going remember to turn off the TV on the treadmill and the loud music on your MP3 so that you can reflect. Remember that having the right behavior is the biggest influencer (and shortcut) to getting what you intended to accomplish.

Many senior directors, including Dominic Barton, the Firm's managing director, go jogging on a regular basis. Some people I know like to engage in even more intense workouts. The key concept is physical activity, which allows you to distance yourself from the current work. Make sure you force yourself to recognize the magic of life: live each and every day to the fullest. It will definitely act positively in your work.

PRINCIPLE 16 Create a Commitment Plan

Do you have a commitment plan? Many people are surprised when I share with them my commitment plan: my long-term vision, mid-term goals, and immediate goals. It's a very useful reminder to set high aspirations. For starters, compartmentalize into four sections: business/career, family, personal health, and friends/network. For each bucket, fill out three or four *outcome or results* oriented phrases (not activities). For example, on my proactive approach to the end of 2016, under business/career, I have written, "Personally mentored and helped 20 people." I have a checkbox next to each item as well. A commitment plan is effective to serve three purposes. One, you become more proactive and achievement driven. Two, you get to measure your progress year after year—adjusting upward or downward but having accountability. Three, you start believing anything is possible and you mean it when you say it. Strangely enough, you start achieving things you've never even dreamed of before. For example, when I wanted an accelerated promotion in 2012, I wrote it down on my commitment plan and achieved it in exactly that time frame, which surprised even my wife.

When you write your commitment plan, deploy a sound structure. For example, you can divide a piece of paper into three horizontal sections across the page. In the first section write how you will achieve each outcome. In the second, write the challenges you are going to face. In the last, write why achieving each result is a must. Then carry this paper with you everywhere you go. It helps you keep focused.

You can also extend your commitment plan ideology to other things. For example, when we write our holiday greetings to our friends and family at the end of the year, we also write another card just for ourselves. On this card, we formally put down what we would have "already achieved" for the following year. This is extremely satisfying and useful when you come back and reread it 365 days later.

Recently, I was in Sydney talking to Internet entrepreneur Peter Bradd, who shared with me a similar practice. Peter is a serial entrepreneur who has launched many different net ventures, most notably Australia's biggest technology incubator coworking space, Fishburners. His commitment plan is on meeting the right kind of people. He said, "It's odd why we are not more selective in who we choose to hang out with. We just kind of hang out with anyone." Peter believes after a certain age, especially after you step into the business world, you should seriously write down the core values, what you like about a person, and actively seek those people out. How many of us have our values and types of people we like written down? It goes to show why someone like Peter has achieved so much at such a relatively young age.

There are many things we can do proactively during our career that we usually only do in a reactionary way. For example, we attend industry-wide information sharing sessions *a few* times a year because it's in our calendars. But if you do only that, how do you expect to forecast future trends, let alone keep up with any trend at all? There should be a smarter way to do so. One method Dave, a McKinsey principal, describes is asking yourself, "When was the last time I . . ." questions. For example, say if you were in the aerospace industry, you might ask yourself, "When was the last time I talked to someone outside my immediate circle?" or "When was the last time I went down to the R&D department below my floor?" or "When was the last time I looked upon a tangential technology?" Our brain works on engagement. Without an approach to feed the brain with the right nutrients, our knowledge will become outdated very quickly. Another method is to keep up a good "scanning habit." We can scan the headlines of our industry and communicate those to peers in our group. Knowledge has a half-life, and if you are not on top, you will be seriously selling yourself short. What if the regulations changed? What if you were the last one to find out? Having a commitment plan focuses your attention on the right activities.

When you start finding your job easier than before, it's usually a warning sign. You may forget what you are missing out on. The danger is that no one will tell you what more you can do if you are doing well "at your current job."

To pursue the leadership track, plan and create your own commitment plan. Within those goals, you will definitely find what you are lacking right now. They will propel you to ask the "right people" question as Pete mentioned or the "When was the last time..." question as Dave suggested. Then make sure you come back to the commitment plan at select intervals such as every six months.

McKinsey consultants have different versions and categories of the same commitment plan. It usually starts in a senior engagement manager period when you are asked to write down your aspirations, client platform, knowledge spike, service-line contributions, and so on. It's not a formal ask but a customary hand-down from past principals who send you their previous drafts. Most consultants start at an even earlier point in their tenures. When ascending from associate to engagement manager, some consultants will choose to write such a plan. These steps give the individuals the important learning opportunities to rethink what is missing and how to rejuvenate their minds.

CHAPTER TWO

Growing with Others

When we take people merely as they are, we make them worse; when we treat them as if they were what they should be, we improve them as far as they can be improved

—J.W. VON GOETHE

We tend to think of becoming a leader as an individual growth journey—you somehow become strong enough to lead others, and then one day others start following you. However, a big chunk of leadership is incomplete without the power to influence and grow other people. At McKinsey, we tend to think of three key stakeholders: clients, other leaders (principals and directors), and team members. Becoming a leader suddenly makes life not about you, but really about satisfying the needs of others.

For me, those needs are in three areas: communication, connection, and understanding

Communication

In communication there are six principles.

PRINCIPLE 17
Always Memorize the First Three Sentences of a Presentation. This is a simple rule that can change the way you come across to everyone in the room.

PRINCIPLE 18
Communicate Using Fewer Words. Learn to say more with fewer words by asking yourself seven key questions for a synthesized delivery.

PRINCIPLE 19
Pause Three Seconds Before Answering Difficult Questions. Don't blurt out an answer immediately; instead show others you can withstand the weight of silence.

PRINCIPLE 20
Question More and Talk Less. Grow by questioning and listening more to other people the way principals and successful entrepreneurs do.

PRINCIPLE 21
Turn No into Yes. Rather than correcting people impulsively, try to help them correct themselves by using suggestive questions.

PRINCIPLE 22
Don't Show Half-Baked Output. Be selective about to whom and when to disclose your end product as your reputation is also on the line.

PRINCIPLE 17 Always Memorize the First Three Sentences of a Presentation

There is a funny experiment about how to give convincing presentations. One research firm took an actor and prepped him up as an expert and made him stand before a client meeting. Afterward, they asked the participants to fill out a survey. They tried it many more times to make sure it wasn't beginner's luck. All surveys showed identical results. People believed he was an expert. He didn't understand a single thing about the subject matter.

Like the actor who fooled the participants into believing he was an expert, there are decisive rules you should follow. One of those is to learn the first three sentences of your presentation by heart.

According to Ulrich, a senior expert at the Firm, the lead-in defines your entire presentation. "When I prepare for new client project pitches, I write down what I say in the beginning and mostly the lead-ins. I make sure I can grab their attention." This is because when you are in the material, people will look at the page on the screen rather than listen to you.

The reason you memorize the first three sentences is because these sentences get the most attention. People are listening and don't fiddle around with their iPhones. If you sound insecure at the beginning of a presentation, people will inadvertently lose interest in you. But the other more important reason is so that it makes *you* feel comfortable. Talent is overrated, especially in public speaking. What's more important is this simple rule that gets you over the nervous edge. When you start from a good flow, you unconsciously create a confident rhythm. You use your accompanying charts to complement your voice but not to dominate. The third impact is on peers who are listening. Senior leaders feel at ease when you display a certain tone and character; team members feel proud.

Most people don't realize this, but what you say in a presentation is completely different from what you put on a page. For example, when a chart is shown on-screen, the brain may immediately process a two-by-two matrix or an XY graph, but you can only explain one axis at a time. There is no way you can capture both axes at the same time and explain them; you need to choose why you will explain a certain side first. Therefore a story always follows a linear path, while a chart with figures may not.

Using shorter sentences can also present you as a more mature leader. When you reach the C-suite level, make your presentation as simple as possible. C-levels and top performers in every field believe that if you sound complicated, you will be complicated. The dilemma is always that when you know a lot you tend to say a lot. Your thought uncontrollably branches outward, and although it makes perfect sense to you, your listeners are lost or bored. Therefore, you need to take a deep breath, recalibrate, and cut down your thoughts. Usually a one-second pause between sentences will enable you to use shorter sentences deliberately.

The attention span of a normal adult is said to be anywhere from 15 to 20 minutes. However, in a business presentation, when the material is more difficult and dry, it's less than 10 minutes.[1] For people talking at professional events, like at TED Talks, the time is even shorter due to higher expectations—the audience is expecting to be amused and aroused every few minutes. The reality is, though, that people have a much shorter attention span—it's in the first few lines. That's why presenters try to come up with a funny anecdote, inspiring quote, or jaw-dropping findings at the onset. The best way to engage people is through emotional connection, and this theory holds true also for memory: greater emotional attachment to a quote, for example, allows you to remember it for a longer time.* Also, remember that the listener's memory, experience, and culture

---

* The dopamine released during an emotional event attaches to the amygdala, the part of the brain responsible for memory and consolidation.

dictate attention deeply. Tailor your message with your audience's background in mind.

Not everyone is a great presenter. I sure wasn't—at first. I usually got very nervous. I still can't speak like my gifted colleagues. But it gets better. Memorizing the first three sentences will help you get that first weight off your shoulders. At least, it will get you off to a good start. Try it and you will see the impact right away.

PRINCIPLE 18 Communicate Using Fewer Words

In my early tenure as an associate, I used to admire people who could imbibe copious amounts of information. The difference became excruciatingly obvious when receiving first-time downloads on a new project. They listen, they comprehend. It was as if these people didn't need to be switched on. Their brains just kept on processing information ad infinitum. Then came the turn for me to not listen but talk. When I started to sell my projects to other consultants to join the team, I learned that processing information was the easier part. You require more brainpower to explain things clearly and effectively than to analyze and understand. Moreover, you realize time is precious for everyone. Thus, the only way to keep your listeners alert is through communicating using fewer words.

McKinsey is the best training ground to learn both push and pull sales—internally. At the Firm, every leader learns exceptional people are hard to come by. When leaders want to "staff"* a specific consultant onto their team, they need to cajole the consultant using clear and attractive value propositions. In other words, they need to be good at pulling people in. On the other hand, consultants learn

---

* At McKinsey, when employees are assigned to a specific project, they are referred as "staffed" onto an engagement.

that if they want to join a project and they don't have enough industry experience, functional expertise, or people network, they need to try very hard to "get in"—the equivalent to a heavy door-to-door push salesperson. Every week, McKinsey consultants receive e-mails showcasing new projects that are about to start. Through a competitive bidding process consultants find their next battleground. It's a simple internal job-hunting world, again and again. Desirable candidates vanish quickly. Others need to wait for the right opportunity. At the core lies a vivid and candid survival-of-the-fittest model.

For ages, since our schooling days, we have been accustomed to selling ourselves into something or somewhere. We apply to competitive universities and, when offered an interview with an alumnus, we try ever so hard to explain why we are an ideal candidate. After graduation, we do the same with our potential employers. We write down our strengths, aspirations, value to the company, and so on. Therefore, it's something you've been trained to do for many years. However, the pull part is relatively new. It's something you acquire at a relatively later time in your business endeavors—when you transition to a leading role.

Talking to someone using fewer words takes practice. It is a lot more difficult than it looks at first because it requires you to order and structure your story clearly, eliminate or omit certain details selectively, choose the right words carefully, and answer potential questions as much as possible in your description. Over the years, I have come up with a list of questions that can guide you in the right direction.

In a nutshell, think through and deliver the following:

1. What do you know already?
2. What do you need to find out at the end of this project or effort?
3. What do you need to ignore or eradicate?

4. What are the constraints and limitations?
5. Who are the key stakeholders and customers?
6. What is the overarching timeline, and what are the important milestones?
7. Why is this project or effort better than anything else? What is the attractive big picture?

By concentrating on convincing people faster and with fewer words, you are building a unique skill. It's like you are becoming the expert anchorman of a well-scripted TV news program. Aim for 30 minutes first and then try saying the same message in half that time (but not through learning to talk faster). Purposely set a time and weigh that against the amount of content delivered. At the same time, see the level of excitement you have generated. This is also your chance to grow as a charismatic leader. If you think about it, most likely, this conversation or discussion will be your first professional engagement (communication) with the other person. Being able to give a dynamic first impression is always a plus.

PRINCIPLE 19 Pause Three Seconds Before Answering Difficult Questions

Questions can be tricky, especially when the stakes are high. You have concerned listeners throw you a maelstrom of tough questions. You have big bosses lurking behind your back. You are nervous and you are trying to impress everyone in the room. Especially when you are facing important C-level executives or high-potential clients, your heart may be racing through the roof. Usually, you are so eager that you want to answer the questions right away. That's where you should purposely hold, wait, and count three seconds.

One of the best pieces of advice I've ever received in my time at McKinsey was to pause before I answered any question. It was already the end of my first year as engagement manager at McKinsey, and I noticed that one of the associate principals in the presentation room always waited for a few seconds, deep in thought, before answering any question. The more difficult those questions got, the more powerful and thought-provoking his answers were.

There are three main reasons why you should pause as well:

1. You have more time to react, think, and come up with the best answer.
2. The listener perceives greater value in your answer by the sheer weight of silence.
3. People tend to overreact in bad or intimidating situations, and pausing is a good way to avoid this.

Framing the major question categories is a great shortcut to stay ahead of your audience. If you are doing a survey, you may remember open- or closed-ended questions, structured or unstructured format. But in a typical setting where questions are raised after a presentation, you can generalize into four buckets: fact-based and information-seeking, discovering, evaluative or comparative, and challenging questions (see Figure 2.1). During a final feedback session with the associate principal, I discussed this with him in more detail. The questions on the left-hand side of Figure 2.1, fact-based and information-seeking questions, are straightforward and should be answered quickly. As you move from those fact-based questions to discovering, evaluative, and finally challenging questions, you can adjust the time you spend answering them. It will not only make you sound a lot more senior and credible but give you the necessary perspective. Examine the typical question samples underneath each category. You've probably figured out that the hardest questions are usually looking for reasons or justification. The common trap people fall into is turning on a defensive strategy. During that study, when the VP of operations challenged us on

TYPE OF QUESTIONS

Fact-based / Information-seeking	Discovering	Evaluative or Comparative	Challenging
• "What is the market share of company X?" • "How many plants are operating under 75% utilization?"	• "What actions do we need to take now? Priorities?" • "If your recommendation is to go digital, what capability do we need?"	• "When you compare the two benchmarks, what are the key drivers of success?" • "How do you assess impact on C?"	• "Why have you not looked into X?" • "Why have you not been able to come up with something more insightful?"

Less difficult   **More difficult**

FIGURE 2.1: Four Types of Questions

why we didn't go down to the factory floor, the associate principal paused and first acknowledged the point out loud. Then he carefully explained the process and approach on how we were planning to carry this out. Instead of stating a confrontational answer—we needed more time, resources, and acceptance of other stakeholders to carry this out—he remained focused on giving a constructive one. The more difficult answer can be passed on offline (and out of the official meeting context), he told me quietly later.

Remember not all questions need answers that are 100 percent correct on the spot. We call this the "art of evasion." I was always very fascinated by senior principals who could answer difficult and challenging questions without sounding awkward. It is a skill that everyone can acquire, but it requires patience and confidence. Normally, the individual asking these challenging questions is not expecting you to come up with answers right on the spot. Knowing what the other person really wants makes a difference in you as a mature leader. Rather than jumping in and coming up with a half-baked solution, it is better to postpone the solution. This is what most senior leaders do best. They use their better judgment and right wording to make it sound better. The last bit is confidence. Sometimes how credible you sound comes from how confident you are. This needs to happen from the minute you walk in the door, and it may be the most important aspect of all.

PRINCIPLE 20 Question More and Talk Less

Have you ever come out of a conversation and felt really great about yourself? Especially after talking to someone amazing and being able to share your heart out?

Well, if I can recall one distinctive commonality between a successful entrepreneur and a principal at McKinsey, it would be that they both question more—and thus listen more—and talk less. This extends out to all the top CEOs in every field—and the people you admire in your field.

The most competent people are the most modest. They'd rather spend the next hour finding out 10 new things from you than telling you about 10 of their past achievements. Logically, that makes a lot of sense. The inquisitive learner gets ahead of everyone because he or she accumulates most in the shortest amount of time. Just to avoid confusion, these questions are not the grilling type of questions asked during a due diligence hearing. These are the inquisitive and thought-adding questions.

Asking questions makes the other person feel great, on top, and empowered. It gives him or her almost a sense of euphoria. I once went into a discussion with a successful Internet entrepreneur who runs a $300- to $400-million company and told him half-jokingly up front, "Today I will ask more questions than you!" However, when the fun dinner ended, I would have to admit, he probably ended up asking more about me, or at best we had 50-50 airtime.

What is it about these successful people that sets them apart? For one, most people never think about the airtime beforehand, and they do. But on a deeper level, the difference is in the nature of their questions, each of which multiplies and induces the next one. For example, it may go like this:

QUESTION (Entrepreneur): "Tell me, what you are doing recently?"

ANSWER (me): I am traveling around working on different projects. A recent one was about building the product development blueprint for a new car.

Q: "Really! Tell me, what is it that you are building?"

A: "We are building the next prototype of a homegrown luxury vehicle based off of a third-party engineering service provider of an Italian sports car maker."

Q: "Wow, what is a third-party engineering service provider?"

A: "Oh, they're companies like Magna Steyr and Lear that make cars for OEMs [original equipment manufacturer: another name for an automotive company]."

Q: "You mean, OEMs don't make cars on their own? I thought they did."

A: "No, it's actually quite common that they outsource some of their vehicle types to third-party contractors."

Q: "That's amazing. So what did you do on this project?"

A: "We helped map out the necessary activities by function and set up quality gates. Basically we jointly helped facilitate the creation of the master plan."

Q: "What's a quality gate?"

A: "It's the gate that OEMs set in differing intervals. To pass it, all the participants in each function of the project need to give a go signal."

Q: "What are some examples?"

And on it goes. Just from this dialogue, there are a few tips worth mentioning:

- First, they do not move from topic to topic. They take a genuine interest in what you are saying and go deeper.
- Second, they are not afraid to admit things they don't know. They do it readily and quickly.
- Third, they are able to grasp the interesting aspect very quickly and follow up with short, clear sentences.

If you can practice holding on, probing things unknown, and grasping interesting ideas and knowledge, you will slowly transform into someone who can *ask more questions and talk less.*

Questioning more enhances your listening skills, no doubt. "Listening is such an underrated talent but extremely important," a senior director and cofounder of the Greater China office said to me in a discussion. "Especially in consulting, where people are trained to always talk, listening is a rare skill to have. Also 70 percent of listening is nonverbal," he added.

It's not just about having the tools to ask questions such as, "Let me try to clarify, what you are really trying to say is 1, 2, 3 . . ." or "Let me synthesize what I've heard in a couple of lines," as we learn when mastering *active listening* techniques, it's having the mindset to spend time and understand the other person. In fact, as the director put it so earnestly, "It is to become fully *available*. Your empathy runs so deep that people don't even realize it."

But for starters, try it out with your friends or colleagues in a casual dinner setting. Just a few weeks ago, I tried it with one of my friends whom I hadn't seen for half a year. He works in the agriculture investment business. We were discussing world hunger and what it would take to feed the planet. I just kept questioning deeper and deeper; boy, he just kept going and going. It was one of the best conversations I'd had in a long while. I learned a lot more than I expected. Immediately on my way home, I received a text from him saying how much fun *he'd* had. I couldn't stop smiling.

Of course, knowing and putting it in practice are two different animals. If you can concentrate from today onward—to question more and talk less—you will be able to unlock many more hidden doors.

PRINCIPLE 21 Turn No into Yes

A Chinese military general and philosopher named Sun Tzu once composed a strategic masterpiece called *The Art of War* for managing conflicts and winning battles, and its thoughts and lessons are widely popularized in our business society today. "Conflicts," he wrote (paraphrased in my interpretation), "allow us to take civilization forward and make progress possible. It may not be avoided."[2] Inevitably, we all live in a world of conflict because it's a necessary evil to get ahead in life. Yet, fast-forwarding 2,500 years from the Spring and Autumn Period of ancient China to the present day, I've learned an alternative way to effectively avoid conflict and still make outstanding progress: refraining from saying no directly and instead asking "suggestive questions."

The role model who endowed me with this concept was a principal named Nao, a gregarious person who has worked in Chicago and Tokyo. His mesmerizing attribute is his method of communication: it's like silky tofu. During internal meeting encounters, he never outwardly criticized or disagreed with me. Yet, when finished, I was somehow left with new input changes and more work to do. He was able to sweep his ideas across the table and implant them in my head without my knowing. It was a smooth work of art, like the movie *Inception* directed by Christopher Nolan, mindfully implanting an idea inside anyone's head, except that I wasn't dreaming or sleeping at all.

Realizing his special talent, I once asked him to take me on a project pitch to a well-known client. Once again, I observed his nodding of approval when the client was saying something quite incorrect about the market. He just patiently listened, but while saying yes he started to slide in suggestive questions like, "I understand, yet, have you ever considered this idea?" or "If we imagine an alternative scenario, what do you think would happen?" or "What if we take out A and B, then what will the market look like?" In a nutshell, he was in fact saying no, but rather than stating it outright, he came back with a question. When the client realized his mistake, he inadvertently corrected it without being embarrassed at all.

Now, why is this so important? Why is it important not to directly oppose anyone outright (and mind you, this is not a cultural sensitivity issue)? Why is it even more important when you rise up the hierarchy—to the senior VP or CXO level?

A few weeks later, over dinner, I approached Nao with my observations. His answer stood out: "First, in most cases you don't need to refute anyone unless it's urgent. It's usually more favorable to indirectly point out a person's mistake and allow him to realize it." Second, no one wants to be denied or told [he or she is] wrong, especially at a higher level, as it impacts their dignity and status. Third, and most important, a conversation is the *most frequent* communication tool and therefore should not be taken so lightly. You should be most sensitive when dealing with potential conflicts."

There are many books written about how to get past someone's no, but perhaps not on controlling your own "no" stance. If you think about it, though, controlling yourself is much easier.

I suspect some people may be confused and take this meaning as being less proactive. It is hardly the case. Proactive does not always mean to be aggressive and state directly what you want. Proactive means to know what you must do to get you there. This technique is just one of the effective ways. Stephen Covey, author of *7 Habits of Highly Effective People*, wrote in another light, "Proactive people aren't pushy. They're smart, value-driven, they read reality, and they know what's needed." He uses the example of Gandhi to portray how one man toppled the British Empire through being proactive in compassion and moral persuasion.[3]

Putting the "suggestive question" technique into practice requires letting your guard down first. Get out of the habit of trying to correct someone impulsively. This is a lot harder than you think because we are so used to asserting the "right" answer. Instead, ask questions that will help other people correct themselves. Step into their world. Have the patience to help them through framing the question in the right way. You need to develop active listening skills and a big picture mindset. Learn to nod more regularly and make an "I see, that's interesting" comment first whenever you disagree, then come up with an alternative question.

Going forward, why not try to slide in more suggestive questions to help your listener agree with you?

PRINCIPLE 22 Don't Show Half-Baked Output

Even with the best of efforts, sometimes you just don't have enough time to meet your deadlines. Clients or customers suddenly want your results the next day for a progress status update, and your senior leader might request a sudden problem-solving session because he has an hour of free time. What do you do? Do you react right away by showing your honest status—current work-in-progress—or hand over something in lieu, like discussion over adjacent matters?

People who shine know when to discuss something. They are careful in choosing when and where to pick their fight. If they know they will look bad, they don't bulldoze and take a chance. The wishful thinking approach usually does not work well in a demanding job environment. Contrary to the conventional axiom of "battles can be lost, but you can win the war," the reality in our complex and competitive environment is that small battles need to be won in order to prove you can win the war. Therefore, be sly and selective. At McKinsey, the weight of one's reputation is significant. When staffing someone on a project, all that's asked is, "How is he or she?" and the reply is not based on a long list of great achievements or faulty mistakes, it's just the reputation that person has in the eyes of our staffing managers and several principals—from comments such as quick, above average, good, or distinctive that they hear after each project. Since decisions are made quickly (especially when projects are abundant), many of us don't go through the hefty due diligence process we are required to do; instead, we take the reputation at face value. As many of us know, bad reputation is hard to change, and bad reputation comes mainly from the perception that you are reckless and half-baked. In other words, good reputation is easier to build if you take good care of your output—only you can control what you show.

When you are a recognized as a leader, people expect you to be on top all the time. You are rated based on your high-quality output, not the input amount of hard work. If you believe it will take you an additional two and a half hours to complete an update, find ways to get that time. Don't get jittery and send out something that is incomplete. "At the higher level, people never trade quality for time efficiency. But too many to-be-leaders fail to see themselves as the last gatekeeper, which is a grave mistake," one engagement manager told me. Securing a way to make the outcome not only in the most desirable content but also in the most desirable timing is also an important part of your growth. Both of these added together, I believe, is the output you should be looking for. Don't settle for anything less.

Connection

In connection there are six principles.

PRINCIPLE 23
Instantly Find a Connection in the Room. Start an important discussion with C-levels by finding some personal thing in common.

PRINCIPLE 24
Be a Giver, Not a Receiver. Become the one who is going to motivate people instead of being motivated all the time.

PRINCIPLE 25
Find the Best Intent in People. Stay positive and forward looking by always finding good things about people and their intent.

PRINCIPLE 26
Learn Team Members' Defining Moments and Personal Sides. Try to get team members closer to you by building a deeper empathy and connection.

PRINCIPLE 27
Think of Everyone as a Helpful Individual, Not a "Resource." Need I say more?

PRINCIPLE 28
Go Out for a Meal with Interesting People Every Week. Make it a deliberate habit to enlarge your current sphere of influence and knowledge.

PRINCIPLE 23 Instantly Find a Connection in the Room

Many of us go into a client's room, an executive's suite, or the boss's office and jump straight into the business at hand. It's safer, we believe, to separate business from other things we do in life. But, "People," Dave, a senior principal, said in the interview, "are more than whatever business problems we are trying to solve." For him, before jumping into any business topic, as an icebreaker, he looks for something in common in the room. "One time I went for a cost-reduction discussion with a U.S.-based automotive company. I quickly glanced through the executive's room and found a picture of a winery in Melbourne, several of them. So I picked it up and began discussing my own winery and bottling challenges back in China." To Dave, finding connections with other people is paramount. At the same time, it is not as difficult as one may think. The amazing thing is that in his 22 years of working in multiple companies, he has yet to find zero connection with any business executive.

When he comes across engagement managers or associate principals acting out the perfectly practiced robot consultant pitch, he quickly tries to bring the matter to a higher level to show them that right context supersedes right content. He believes this skill needs to be developed over time and requires a conscious or deliberate effort to find the best connection available in the room. Multiple things, outlined in many of the principles throughout the book, can help you increase your chances of connecting with people. For example, you have to be curious about meeting interesting people. You may need to increase your hobbies, especially picking up certain art, music, or craft interests enjoyed by top-level leaders. When traveling, maybe you should not limit to just sightseeing but engage in local activities and immerse in local cultures. But these are just some surface suggestions. What really matters is constant awareness to reach greater intimacy.

On one occasion, Dave went to meet another client, a CTO of a major manufacturer. He purposely did not bring his notebook, pen, or laptop. His purpose was just to sit down and talk. Over the years, he has learned that every time you go to a meeting with a thing in your hand, you become more guarded and the other person more expecting. He wanted to try out a new method. It took a lot of courage, he admits. "We are so used to having something to show," he said. But the CTO then shared with him many of the issues that were never unearthed in his previous meetings. For him, it was a new type of intimate connection based on clearing the atmosphere, filling it with the client's concerns, and learning to be a plain good listener. This is another example of finding connections beyond the normal business transactions.

As you shape your next leadership path, focus on *how you can connect* with other high-level like-minded people through finding connections in the room.

PRINCIPLE 24 Be a Giver, Not a Receiver

I have a favorite quote from the late Maya Angelou that fits perfectly with this occasion: "Try to be a rainbow in someone else's cloud." She was a rainbow in many people's minds.[4]

On a particularly crummy day, when you felt a bit unmotivated to work, do you remember being saved by a few words?

- "What's wrong, do you want to take a bit of a rest?
- "You seem a bit down today, what's troubling you?"
- "Where's that energy I usually see beaming from you?"

Until a certain point in your professional career, it's still all right to be the one being cheered on. You are still the apprentice and in training. However, from a certain point onward, that has to change. That point of inflection is when you transition to a leadership role. You are no longer the receiver of these caring and empathizing questions, you are the giver. Learn to find a physical place every day before you arrive to work to reset your professional mindset to the "mood maker" and "giver." It may be the revolving doors when you enter your office building, or it may be when you put your jacket on. Even in situations when you are under a lot of stress, you will need to train yourself to keep calm and put on a smile in front of your team members. Part of maturity as a leader comes through this conscious effort.

Picture someone with great energy: a role model, a mentor, or even a mature colleague. Start emulating this person now. Start asking why he or she is able to radiate energy differently from others all the time. During one project, I realized that Henry, an entrepreneur turned engagement manager, never lost his optimistic energy. It didn't matter how beat we were in progress reviews; he bounced right back up with questions such as, "What a ride, where do we go next?" and "Who should we tap into to get additional directions?" His focus was constantly on giving energy to others and pushing things forward to the next level. "Ah but . . ." you might say, "that's normal, given his role." And, yes, that's true—well, half true. You could also say he was very conscious about it. Most people are not made up of these ingredients in the first place. Later, as that leader moved on to become the right-hand man of UBS, a global investment giant, in Taiwan, I realized his giving aura got even brighter—even now, after leaving the firm, he gives weeks of training at McKinsey on his own time. I believe the good news here is yes, you need to become the giver and mood maker as you transition to leadership, but when you master them, those skills and that mindset stick with you the rest of your life.

But sometimes these emotions build up. Even when you must act in a certain way, you want a place to discharge your frustrations. How can that be done? One way is to use the "withdrawal approach." It means to take yourself out of the current situation and look at it from a third-person perspective. This way you can see more objectively where you are and what is causing your negative mood. Other ways are to talk to someone you trust or to write it down. This will get the issue off your chest and alleviate your worries for the time being.

PRINCIPLE 25 Find the Best Intent in People

Work is not fun if you do not work with people you enjoy. This is often very hard to do. Why? Well, we each have our own differences, and we rarely get the chance to choose people we work best with. One of the trade secrets I discovered at McKinsey was finding the best *in* people and not necessarily finding the best people to work with every time.

McKinsey does project-oriented work. This means we come together for one project, disband, and then go for another, disband, and so forth. Therefore, until a certain point in your career it is very difficult to choose, really, anything. Even when you become an engagement manager, teams are handpicked by principals or associate principals at least half of the time.

During my first project I had an extremely intolerable associate on the team who had just joined the Firm. He had an elite track record at his previous government job but, for some reason, was extremely insecure and strange. To give you an example, during one of our progress reviews, he intentionally told me to stay out and *locked me* out of the conference room—to this day I am unsure why. He saw me standing outside the glass doors and didn't budge (it was at an angle where others couldn't see). My engagement manager at the time was also underwater, so I had to take it upon myself to fix the problem. So what did I do? Knowing I couldn't change the team dynamics, unsure of whom to talk to, not wanting to be seen as an issue raiser from my first year, and also disliking face-to-face confrontation, I decided to take the matter in the only way possible: I decided to think that he had some form of positive intent—that he had the best interest of me, the project, and the outcome at heart. It was the only option given that I had no one else to turn to. He had been hired by McKinsey's rigorous selection process, and I had to trust the system or it would imply I would not trust McKinsey. Yet this action and thinking transformed me into a different person.*

Throughout my McKinsey career, my feedback always had a sentence or two praising me for having an "overwhelmingly positive attitude about others." It really didn't matter whether the person was a client, a team member, or a principal, most of the time I tried to see the positive qualities in everyone. Seeing them in this light made me feel positive about life.

When I meet someone, I am usually amazed by our differences. But I know human beings relate better when we search for commonalities. This is the first step I learned. I search for commonalities quickly. Just the other day, during a semiformal dinner with seven new people, I overheard two different people talking about commonalities and exchanging contacts right away. If no immediate commonality exists, I look for whatever amazes me most about the person and make it something I want to be interested in in the future.

Some things that you may find negative about someone, others would not. If someone is too aggressive to be given airtime during a presentation, one might perceive it as "He is passionate and helpful," while others might take it as "He is obnoxious and annoying." I

---

* In my interviews, I learned that many people (engagement managers to directors alike) had shared a similar point of view. It is important not only to be positive at work but to believe others have positive intent. This is important because miscommunication happens and good intentions can go awry when working in a very demanding and high-paced environment. Indra Nooyi, PepsiCo chairman and CEO, said, "Whatever anybody says or does, assume positive intent. You will be amazed at how your whole approach to a person or problem becomes very different," as quoted in *Fortune*, "The Best Advice I Ever Got (25 CEO/Leaders)."

try to take the former view every time. The emphasis people put on perception, though unknowingly and subconsciously, is a serious mind barrier. Therefore you need to pay attention and a get a grip on the destructive and criticizing nature of the mind.

Another example: Think about rain. A farmer coming out of a dry season would leap for joy, but someone who had planned a hiking weekend, maybe not. Therefore, depending on your expectations, the perceived outcome and appreciation is extremely different.

There are a few immediate mindset changes you can do now to find the best in people:

1. Take things on a positive spin.
2. Remember only the great things about a person.
3. Build positive attitude through appreciating small things.
4. Be curious, thinking, "that's interesting," not judgmental.
5. Ignore differences.

So what else did I find in this intolerable associate? I discovered he was extremely hardworking. Rather than spending five minutes fixing a printer problem, he would spend that time working on another slide. He seemed much more dedicated to delivering high-impact work than I was at that time. He went back relentlessly to his client counterpart to gather the right facts for his process flow chart. He came across as someone who never called it quits. His persistence was admirable.

PRINCIPLE 26 Learn Team Members' Defining Moments and Personal Sides

One day, 20 or so of my colleagues received a secret invitation to a short leadership training. The invitees came from varying tenures from engagement manager to senior director, a setup that was rare for the Firm. As prework we were given an assignment to write up—a short life essay, like an MBA essay, describing our turning points, major losses, dreams, and life stories—to enhance our learning experience. That morning, we gathered around in a U-shaped fashion and the coaches started pairing us up in front of the participants. The next moment, the coaches handed each person an essay and asked us to read it out loud. It came as a shock to everyone. Sensitive personal stories such as a divorce, painful illness, and childhood trauma flooded the meeting auditorium. It was indeed a unique and powerfully engaging experience. Reading these heartfelt essays brought the person to real life.

Upon some reflection, a colleague and I discovered we hardly knew each other. Although we had meals together, talked about our challenging projects, and had even taken a small trip together, we had seemingly passed over these personal details. We shrugged our shoulders, realizing that we had never really talked.

At work we tend to avoid these conversations as we keenly try to separate our personal and professional lives. Even just recently, I met up with an old alumnus, my engagement manager who transferred from New Jersey to Hong Kong, and found that his family was from Taiwan. Back in 2009, I worked with him on a five-month project as a business analyst, yet I did not know where his family was from. I was baffled. He said, "Oh yeah," smiling teasingly, "I guess you never asked." What the leadership exercise told us was that we were able to bond much closer given the right set of tools and atmosphere. After those few days, all 20 or so of us, including senior directors and younger tenured engagement managers, started clicking. Plato, a Greek philosopher, once said, "You can discover more about a person in an hour of play than in a year of conversation." This was the first time I experienced playing out our lives in front of an audience without a stage. Imagine the scene again. One participant starts crying realizing how tough a long-distance relationship has been on her marriage. In another, a participant tells about his lost connections with his father. When it was our turn to be read, we felt nervous, happy, and scared at the same time. It was a sensation we hadn't felt since middle school or high school—we were completely vulnerable and free-floating in midair. I learned that setting aside time to gain meaningful engagement experience with people brings outstanding results.

Sharing such stories with your work cohorts will be challenging. Nevertheless, staged or unstaged, it's important to bring our defining moments out and improve the day-to-day connection we have with one another. Top-notch companies spend millions of dollars each year to improve connection. Executives in companies like Starbucks also realize this goal by giving specific employee training focused on how to overcome adversity—dealing with angry customers in its case.[5] Sheryl Sandberg said in *Lean In* that she, too, has evolved from putting on the professional persona to showing her personal side: "I think we benefit from expressing our truth, talking about personal situations, and acknowledging that professional decisions are often emotionally driven." This works to your advantage. Had she declined an attractive offer from Larry Summers at the Treasury using professional reasons and not her personal divorce reasons (D.C. brought back painful memories), she probably could not have called Larry so swiftly when she wanted to get back in.[6] Her prudence and personal honesty made this transition possible. Thus, it is important to realize what is at the bottom of all this: empathy. People are moved by feeling for others. As you grow into a leader, the understanding of people's will, motivation, and emotions becomes a more important factor.

Think about the will and skill matrix for a moment. It's a two-by-two matrix used to gauge a person's level of skill and will. The horizontal axis is influenced by practical skill enhancement. The vertical axis is the level of will. Skill is important, but the will gets the work done. Thus, influencing the will is a better return for time and output for most managers. Moreover, research has consistently shown that willpower is a better predictor of a person's success, and hence of a project's success—and your success as a leader. Thus, bonding with your team members with personal stories will allow the team to work with the necessary trust and desire to contribute to a higher cause.

PRINCIPLE 27 Think of Everyone as a Helpful Individual, Not a "Resource"

No one wants to be treated like a "resource." Why then is it hard to avoid this? There are some obvious reasons. We live in a corporate pyramid-based hierarchy, and the culture of the organization makes it normal. People can easily be substituted. So the list goes on. What allows you to break this spell?

I believe there are four things you can do.

- **Use a leveraging mindset.** At McKinsey, people always use the term, "I'll leverage so and so." There is a big difference in mindset between reporting versus leveraging. One principal said to me that when you are reporting you see one vertical line that points upward, versus when you are leveraging the lines are interconnected like a web. It's a mentality that needs to be nurtured from early on.

  For example, on one cross-border project between China and Canada, I asked one of my associate principals to return to the office at 11 P.M. because we were under a lot of time pressure to finish the deck. He was out on a client dinner but happily returned to help create a couple of charts on a particularly important communication section to the CEO. In the end, we were able to complete the deliverables on time by the next morning.

When you leverage someone, your mindset is in the "I am being helped" mode. Likewise, when someone is leveraging you, you will share an equal feeling. It's important to have this distinction from the onset.

- **Go into the trenches.** A lot of times our credibility is determined by how dedicated we are to the people we work with. The higher up you go, the more people will care about your actions and not just your leadership strategy. Thus, it is always important to get your hands dirty and to present yourself as someone who can go into the trenches. Take the lead in doing something cumbersome. Focus on being the first one to have a crack at hard problems. Stand up frequently to write on whiteboards. Aggressively seek your team members out for lunch and ask how they are doing. "The key for me is that I never leave the problem-solving session without making certain the team is comfortable to work on it themselves. I never quit halfway," said Laurent, a principal who has worked in four different countries. When you are already the one in the trenches, aggressively engaging in creating the output, you no longer need to worry about the individual versus resource question.

- **Make the person feel as if only she or he can do, if possible.** The most rewarding way is to make the person feel special. The way to carry this out effectively is not hard. You just need to remember to add in the beginning or the end of your discussion why you believe this to be ideal for the person. It's really about keeping the person excited about the topic. There is one extra facet to achieving this, however. You need to know what the individual cherishes deep down. The best time to get such information is over a meal. Rather than discussing the project or any trivial matters, you can use this time to dig out what the person uniquely excels at.

- **Say and show "thank you."** As intuitive as this may seem, it's unbelievable how often we forget such a simple act of courtesy. Gratitude is the easiest way to treat individuals as individuals and yet the hardest thing to deliver for some. I have time and again witnessed many leaders who couldn't say a simple thank you at the work we did for them. It not only makes you feel worthless but also makes you want to avoid working with such an individual. Some people say that professional relationships do not require gratitude, that it is a sign of giving concession to the people below. No, it's the opposite. This thinking is only true if you think the person who is following your orders is solely an object for exploitation, a tool or resource. It is imperative that you give the other person credit. It's professional etiquette.

Show gratitude not just by writing it in e-mails. Make sure the other person hears you loud and clear. Choose the occasion carefully, too. If you can, try to give people words of praise in front of people that matter most to them.

PRINCIPLE 28 Go Out for a Meal with Interesting People Every Week

When I was an associate at the Firm, the best advice I got from a senior principal was to take the time to go out with amazing people, even if that meant postponing work until 3 A.M. He was very keen on the development of the mind, especially during your twenties and early thirties.

There is a saying about how great a book is: if a book has one passage or one idea to change a person's life, that alone justifies reading it and rereading it. If you meet a person who can share with you any idea or saying that makes you think and rethink again, then it justifies taking the time to meet with him or her. One of the prime reasons for meeting more people is to enlarge your mental capacity. From your late twenties you can clearly start seeing trends of young leaders—leaders showing mental complexity similar to a fifty-year-old's. Moreover, Robert Keegan and Lisa Lahey, professors and researchers at Harvard University, write, "Increased mental complexity and work competence, assessed on a number of dimensions, are correlated. . . . Growth correlates with effectiveness for CEOs and middle managers."[7]

Recently, I met with a professor who teaches creative writing, a young hedge fund manager, and a friend who works for Google. From each, I learned at least one valuable lesson. The discussion with the professor taught me to become more creative and resilient in chasing opportunities, especially when odds are tough. This bright professor earned his PhD via long-distance learning in the U.K. while raising two children, working full-time as a translator, and publishing several books to boost his credentials. Compared to consulting, the hedge fund industry is focused on meeting targets. According to my hedge fund manager friend, "As long as you hit target, you can be doing anything you want," which is very different from a client-facing profession such as consulting. Therefore, if you like a more black-and-white "results"-driven job, a job as a hedge fund manager will better suit you. I was pleasantly surprised to learn that Google was an even more people-oriented company than McKinsey. I had always thought Google was more technocratic—focused on just gadgets and product innovation—than anything else.

For each encounter, write out key questions:

- What is fun and rewarding about what you do?
- What is your vision? How did you get there?
- What's new and interesting recently? Or, what interesting things have caught your attention?

Meeting interesting people does not come easy. It takes patience, especially if you are not used to this habit. Therefore, you need to create a sound structure that can change your current behavior. Below are some easy-to-follow guidelines to make this habit easier to surface:

- Start with someone close.
- Create your own filter by industry, function, interests, age range, and so on.
- Go to your e-mail account, open your contact list, and start writing a few e-mails to people you haven't met for more than a few months. Sunday morning is a good time for this.
- Choose a day out of the week that has the highest probability of your success. For me, Thursdays work best to get people's time. Wednesdays are usually the busiest, and Fridays are reserved for personal or more informal dinners.
- Prepare at least one pivotal question or theme you are dying to know from this person as well as something you would like to share with him or her.
- Keep it a continuous exercise rather than a one-off—don't let occasional cancellations stop you; it really does happen.
- Don't come out of the chat with a rating such as "That was really A," or "That was just a waste of time". At the same time, don't rate yourself either.

One rewarding way to keep up is to summarize your thoughts on paper after the meeting. I carry around a small notebook. After I say my goodbyes, I just quickly sit down and take fifteen minutes or so to sum up what I've learned. You preserve a vivid story that way.

Understanding

In understanding there are five principles.

PRINCIPLE 29
Consciously Gauge Your People. Turn into a great people-reader by analyzing team members' process, problem analysis, will, collaboration, and past performance.

PRINCIPLE 30
Assign Team Members Meaningful Tasks. Provide opportunities to grow by giving independent, challenging, and reward-driven tasks.

PRINCIPLE 31
Create Followership Through Deliberate On-the-Job Coaching. Coaching team members is one of the most effective ways to create followership.

PRINCIPLE 32
Deliver Feedback Using Positive Criticism. Delivering criticism does not have to be harsh when you use a simple technique.

PRINCIPLE 33
Please Your Assistant and Support Staff. Assistants and support staff are crucial to your success; treat them with uttermost care.

PRINCIPLE 29 Consciously Gauge Your People

How do you decide how much work someone can do? Is there a standard way to do this? Why are some people really great at reading others? What is behind this power?

As you transition to a leader you must become a great people reader. It is really what sets you apart from others. Cultivate the antenna to gauge your team members' capacity to complete small, medium, and large tasks, the quality and the quantity.

Have you ever had an experience where you said to yourself, "If I knew how much additional trouble this person would bring, I would have done that task on my own!"? I am sure you have banged your head on the wall (or slammed your computer) once, twice, or more for this unnecessary "double work." Being annoyed by an incompetent team member is your worst nightmare. But the question is, who is incompetent? You or your team member?

Like the saying, "If the listener is confused, it is usually the speaker's lack of clarity and not the listener's lack of understanding," the leader of projects and people has to use the same yardstick to assess his or her situation. Here are four core questions to keep in mind:

- Are you asking the team member to do the right thing?
- Are you being careful and clear enough on the end output deliverables?
- Have you estimated the correct deadline? Or, were you too optimistic?
- Have you factored in all the potential roadblocks?

Most of the time, the greatest value a leader can bring is to slice and dice the problem and necessary activities into bite-size pieces so that it is in an understandable language. You adjust. You tailor. Not the other way around. You need to learn to bring out this skill naturally.

From my experience, there are five guiding angles to keep in mind when you look at gauging people effectively. Below are the cues:

1. Process. How well does the individual multitask? Can he or she eliminate and prioritize work quickly? Does the individual create a work plan and stick with the agreed timeline?
2. Problem analysis. How well can the individual conduct analysis? What are his or her technical skills? How much guidance and correction would you need to give?
3. Will/attitude. Does the individual go beyond what is asked? How eager is the individual to learn?
4. Collaboration mindset. How mature is the individual? Is he or she a positive influence to the team and client?
5. Past performance. Does the individual have major flaws? Is he or she improving at a great speed?

To conduct a reality check on items 1 through 4, try the following actions:

- **Give mini-tasks.** It is important when you ask someone to do any menial task, for example, to print a document out, that you carefully observe. Does the person come out with the appropriate page format? Does he ask you what you want first? Does he get two versions ready if the desired format is unclear? All of these are clues for you to see how thoughtful he is.
- **Spend enough time with each person in the first few days.** Take quick notes in the first few days. It helps you avoid unwanted double work when you are well into the project—when you will need your team member to get up to speed quickly. Also, don't forget to observe the person's personality on top of his or her talent. When the project is under duress, a team member with a good heart can go a long way.

PRINCIPLE 30 Assign Team Members Meaningful Tasks

During one feedback discussion a few years back, a junior engagement manager reflected on the difficulty of assigning tasks. Gauging, as discussed in the previous section, is the prerequisite, but there is a sound rule on how to give meaningful tasks.

Giving team members meaningful tasks not only makes your job easier, it makes your output better. There is a smart saying I learned from one of the senior principals early on as an engagement manager: he said, "If you were to write an e-mail directing your team member to do something, the effort and time it takes to deliver that task should be at least greater than three times the time it took for you to write that e-mail. Anything else, you try to do it yourself." Of course, there is no telling on the actual time, but the point is clear. Meaningful tasks are tasks that will take time and effort. They will have impact.

When you think back to what makes you happy about working on a task, it usually boils down to only a few factors. First, you were able to solve a problem or challenge by yourself, like riding a bicycle without support wheels as a child. Second, what you accomplished wasn't easy. That's why when you learned to ride your bicycle you tend to remember that moment for the rest your life. Third, people around you and above you recognized your accomplishments—the task should be meaningful enough that it deserves recognition. You must have felt above the clouds when other little kids at the park looked in awe at your new bicycling skills while your parent and other adults congratulated you. So in giving assignments, tasks that are meaningful are a combination of independently cut out, difficult, and recognized work.

How do you go about carving out independent, difficult, and challenging work that will deserve recognition after it's completed?

Independent work:

- Is self-standing work that does not overlap with that of other team members (e.g., has clear accountability and ownership)
- Enables a person to give presentations or lead discussions as a sole agenda point in a meeting
- Does not need to wait for another person's data or output to finish the job
- Can be done individually and not in the same room

Difficult and challenging work:

- Has a clear solution or end outcome, but how to get there is not transparent
- Is outside the person's comfort zone
- Is new or semi-new
- Fits the phrase, "I need to put in some time to think about it"
- Would make you excited if you were to do it

Recognized work:

- Has clear impact, both to the customer and to internal discussions
- Is distinctive, thought-provoking, and real
- Is universally thought of as being great—like learning how to play a song on the piano

When giving meaningful tasks, you need to be mindful of all three facets and also make sure each individual understands how his or her work fits into the overall picture. When we are busy crafting the end output image, we tend to forget that all of our coworkers minds are not synced up like a computer connected to a network. When you remember to explain the entire picture, team members will not only appreciate your compassion but also apply their best efforts to produce better output.

Lastly, give the spotlight to others whenever possible. During our final progress review with an auto client, the principal made sure to make known that the strong implications coming out from the regression analysis were due to my push to collect inventory data from all 80-plus warehouses. However, I made a following comment: the analysis was possible because of one analyst's tenacious efforts downloading gigabytes of data. I made sure the client recognized his hard work. The importance can't be overstated: have the heart to recognize team members' work not just to the internal team and department heads, but all the way to the end client. It's up to you as a leader to give the right recognition. Choose wisely, but not sparingly.

PRINCIPLE 31 Create Followership Through Deliberate On-the-Job Coaching

Followership is vital in any leadership position. As you ascend through the higher ranks, it's something that makes people envious. There are several words that are associated with the ability to create followers: *inspirational, charismatic, innovative, passionate, distinctive,* and so on. Many are hard to attain even over time, and some are hard to attain at all. However, one element—the deliberate act of coaching—can have a huge impact on creating followership. The good news is that you can do it too.

I had a life-changing engagement manager, Ulrich, on my first study in Shanghai. He was a meticulous, caring, and adventurous fellow, doing outward engagements in China. He came into the office one weekend to teach another analyst and me how to create financial models. He meant it as joke when he approached us for a free training session on the weekend. We both shouted "Yes!" to his surprise. On the coming Saturday, he met up with us from 10

A.M. to 6 P.M. and took us through a full module—he used to teach financial modeling back in Germany. Later that night we celebrated our passion for learning jointly; it was a lot of fun. These kinds of stories are often heard at the Firm. Senior leaders openly free up their time to do more for the greater good of the colleagues at the Firm. This is because leaders know that cultivating the leaders of tomorrow is imperative for the Firm's success and hence their own success.

Indeed, taking the initiative and time to do something for someone is easier said than done. Especially if you are a busy leader with nonstop tasks to run, on-the-job coaching, unless required, sounds like a tough luxury to afford. Even if you weren't that busy, it rarely makes sense to spend your precious time coaching others whom you may never get a chance to work with again.

In a subsequent interview with Ulrich a few years later, he said, "Ultimately, helping people learn gives me back a lot of energy. By coaching, you not only increase the day-to-day output as a team, but also learn about the depth of the subject." To succeed as a leader anywhere, you need apprenticeship. Moreover, you want your apprentice to share the same values as you do. Creating that right mindset is done through deliberate coaching. It's practical and personally rewarding.

Another principal told me a major part of his on-the-job coaching was to schedule talks about non-work-related questions—career- or interest-related development goals. He created a standard format to fill in team members' long-term aspirations, strengths, study goals, and development needs in one neat binder. He would come back to it every two to three weeks with each individual of the team. This way, he says, you can keep track of the interactions and help team members find meaning in their jobs. For instance, if an associate is interested in education and the project is about fixed cost reductions for an automotive company, it may be hard for the individual to stay motivated. In such situations, he tries to find meaning by trying to link some aspect of education, such as a training and capability building workshop, to build the associate's interest. He believes that this is the only way to stay genuinely interested in each individual and also understand what makes each one tick.

Ulrich takes pride in developing others. He has helped many junior consultants transform into mature leaders. The type of followership he created really lasts a lifetime. I still turn to him when I need his help. In return, I feel like I have to do everything to help him out, should he require my assistance. It's been already five years since we worked together, and we are miles apart, but the relationship continues. That's something unique you can create through on-the-job coaching.

PRINCIPLE 32 Deliver Feedback Using Positive Criticism

Usually when you have little time, you tend to give quick, terse, and direct feedback. Of course hurting someone's feelings is not your intention. However, my stance on leadership is simple. Happy and positive people will like you. It's like the song, "Row, row, row your boat gently down the stream, merrily, merrily, merrily, life is but a dream," you sang way back in preschool. Life's too short to be critical all the time: "Eighty percent of the time we [automatically] are talking about what went wrong. So I try to focus on how to communicate the negative better as much as possible," Laurent, a principal discussed earlier, told me.

In any situation, there is a way to communicate serious feedback without sounding harsh. The last thing you want from anyone, especially during an ongoing project, is a dejected and demotivated will. Therefore, you should always deploy the ingenious "positive criticism technique." Here's an example of how it works:

- "James, your recent regression analysis was really something. The client was blown away at how we identified inefficient warehouses." (*Positive start*)
- "Yet, I couldn't help but notice the mistake made when transferring that onto our presentation, where I had to go back and forth with Excel and output to make sure all errors were gone." (*Criticism*)
- Here you wait for James to give you some form of explanation.
- "Next time, I suggest you print everything out and recheck all your figures." (*Actionable recommendation*)
- "But hey, how you delivered your results in front of Ajay was excellent, I think that delivery is truly distinctive." (*Positive end*)

Here is how the simple logic works. You praise first. Then you convey the meat of the correction. Lastly, you end with more praise. Often the praise does not have to be directly related to the problem at hand. It can be from something trivial such as, "I really like how you are able to help secure the team room and time for everyone in advance." This method has significant impact. It does not take much mental stress or time. I believe it is time well invested because the receiver will come out with two pluses and one minus. You want team members to always have the positive energy to confront any situation.

Why is this kind of feedback important? And why should you care about it?

Pop quiz: What does a CEO spend most of his time doing on his job? Did you know that at least half of a CEO's job is about finding the right talent? That implies talent is sacred. Having better and more talented people increases your competitiveness. Almost half a year ago, I was talking to an alumnus who is now the GM of merchant sales for eBay in China. Still quite new to his role and job, he told me that he was so surprised how he spends more than 60 percent of his time managing motivation and drafting attractive ways to get candidates. That is exactly what top consulting and investing firms spend billions of dollars doing. However, the second implication and the real question you should be asking yourself is, how can you nurture talent?

At McKinsey, the emphasis on feedback and professional development is especially strong. This is because we believe all consultants "graduate" and become "alumni" of the firm and go on to do great things in life—recall that 1 out of 690 McKinsey alumni become CEOs of public companies. But even outside of this consulting index, there is direct benefit to nurturing growth. If a CEO's job is to find talent, and you know that great talent is scarce, you need to know how to invent talent. Virtually every time you are writing your three-hour feedback report or providing positive criticism, you are investing your learning into how you grow talent.

PRINCIPLE 33 Please Your Assistants and Support Staff

Booking meeting rooms, finding great restaurants, setting up meetings, scheduling and rescheduling calls, and more, there are tons of logistical errands to run at work. The worst thing is that no one *really* appreciates support staff for doing a great job. It's taken for granted. If you do a poor job, and one strike is all it takes, people think you are lousy and incompetent. The risk of failing is enormous. Let an expert handle this.

Getting your assistants on board requires making them happy. Spend the time to run down the major content and context of your projects with staff members. Every few weeks it is best to engage them through a sit-down discussion. On my engagements I tried to have a kickoff meeting with assistants. During the first week or as early as possible, spend a full hour explaining your project scope. I always invited the three or four core assistants on every project into one meeting room and offered them popular sweets while I did the talking. They were really happy so that even after the project ended they continuously extended their support to help me on many other trivial matters.

Out there in the academic world, there are rich and abundant studies run by psychologists on social, emotional, and practical intelligence—for starters, read books by Daniel Goleman. These studies investigate why people get what they want through knowing what to say, how to say it, and at what timing. One of the most obvious ways is to provide people with a bigger picture of the project situation and not use a piecemeal approach. Of course, you may think it's wasting your valuable time to give important information about what you wish to achieve out of the project or what the expectations are for the project. Yet, when you share some of your goals of the project with the assistants, they are more than willing to help you out when you need them to. Some principals go as far as sharing their "to-do" lists.

If you make this your habit, chances are staff members will help you with almost anything. I once was moved by one assistant because she would help me book team rooms every time I came back from the client site. I didn't need to say anything. She studied my schedule and put those in automatically. Later, when we had an end-of-the-project barbecue out by the marine park, all of the assistants showed up. My team members were surprised, and one said, "It's the first time I saw so many people show up!" This is the power you will need well beyond your project leader capacity; it is a huge way to attract people.

So from next time keep this in mind. The best investment you can make is to treat your team assistant and executive's assistant with respect and care. Bring them souvenirs from your business trip. Treat them with an expensive tiramisu.

Here are a few additional reminders:

1. Prepare souvenirs that are nice. Be sure to give them something they will know right away.
2. Set up a formal session to go through your project objectives early in the study.
3. Invite staff members to official team dinners and gatherings.
4. Learn details of their family so you can do something more for them next time.

Start this habit early, and as you ascend to the higher echelon of the hierarchy, make sure you get better and better at it.

CHAPTER THREE

Excelling in Process Management

Productivity is never an accident. It is always the result of a commitment to excellence, intelligent planning, and focused effort.

—PAUL J. MEYER

Process management is the anchor for impact. When you think of process, what words come to your mind? Path? Flow? Value chain? The nature of any work we do involves some form of process: "Why is this done in this way?" and "How can I make this even better?" Typically, when we look at process we look for cues such as ease of implementation, proof of time-efficiency, and indication of results.

In the last two sections we studied how to build the self and grow with others. These were focused on the mindsets and capabilities of you and others. In this section, I want to present key productivity themes and enablers in process management.

Productivity Themes and Enablers

PRINCIPLE 34

Always Prepare an Agenda Before Meetings. An agenda is an important priority-setting process, and it must be presented.

PRINCIPLE 35

Create "Four Boxes" To Dos. Optimize your to dos by dividing them up into four different sections: current work, this week new engagements, personal, and new learning.

PRINCIPLE 36

Focus on Outcome Not Activities. To focus on outcome and results, introduce a check-in and check-out policy.

PRINCIPLE 37

Know Your Meeting Modes in Advance. Segment your meeting categories in advance to preempt all the preparation work beforehand.

PRINCIPLE 38

Proactively Manage E-mail Communication Using the 5D Rules. Delegate, delete, defer, deword, and deactivate to enjoy a healthier e-mail-free lifestyle.

PRINCIPLE 39

Speak up as Early as Possible. Master the six peripheral speaking opportunities to be part of the discussion.

PRINCIPLE 40

Create a Minimalist Presentation Tool Kit. Memorize the six core charts that make up a presentation backbone structure.

PRINCIPLE 41

Create an Easy-to-Use Template for Updates. Always have a template for updates and make sure you involve everybody in your communication loop.

July 18 Agenda: 2:30 – 5:30

Topic	Facilitator		
	Presenter	Support	Time (mins)
• Share current situation and root cause from quick scan and discuss roadblocks, immediate fix, and required additional resources.	xxx	xxx	10
• Performance management	xxx	xxx	30
• Initiative and campaign	xxx	xxx	30
• By branch financial performance	xxx	xxx	30
• Decide owners and location for prioritization workshop	xxx	xxx	10
• Balance between short-term and mid- to long-term	xxx	xxx	15
• Focus area for global expansion program based on outcome	xxx	xxx	15
• Discuss actions for August 8 conference workshop	xxx	xxx	30
• Q&A and next step	xxx	xxx	10

FIGURE 3.1: Agenda

PRINCIPLE 34 Always Prepare an Agenda Before Meetings

Always prepare an agenda for internal and external discussions. If you are not in charge, ask whether your counterpart has prepared one. If not, you should quickly stand up and write the agenda before the meeting starts or in the first five minutes.

Some might be bothered to ask, why raise such a straightforward thing? Fair point. It's because after so many projects outside of McKinsey, I realized many meetings lack an agenda. It sounds unbelievable, but it's true. Especially, people ignore the importance of an agenda when the meeting is small. This is when you need structure the most. Without an agenda, you have time overruns, lack of focus, and unhappy people across the room.

A sample agenda can look like Figure 3.1.

Writing an agenda is a top-down process. It's a commitment. Often we don't pay particular attention to the value—an agenda is often "just there" by someone—but it's an important priority-setting process. When you make your own agenda you need to pay particular attention to the wordings and the outgoing message being communicated. That's why corporate CEOs make sure they "Set the agenda" loud and clear on their mission statement memorandum. On a day-to-day level, an agenda is crucial for a few noteworthy reasons:

1. Having an agenda helps you avoid missing important points in case discussions become heated. Many people have a limited attention span beyond three or four sentences. It is harder to concentrate on a speaker especially when there are three other meetings to go to or an urgent document due in several hours. Normally, after you run through the agenda it is important to ask, "Have I missed any important points during this meeting?" and quickly get everyone's alignment. This avoids the expectation gap, especially when one is going into a meeting with rather hostile discussions.

2. It empowers you to skip to an interesting section when the listeners are bored. Oftentimes, due to many external factors, a meeting does not go as planned. There are usually, however, a few sections you need to cover to get input during the meeting and others where you can follow up later. During an important steering committee with the domestic sales head of a major automaker, for example, we quickly learned that he was impatient. We needed to communicate that some factories were underperforming and underutilized, causing major losses for the company. Instead of going through the step-by-step workshop method of addressing the issue, showing the analysis with facts, and synthesizing the "so what" implications, we took him directly to the recommendation and action plan. This way, if he wanted to know the reason, we were able to go back to a particular slide in a flash; otherwise, we wanted input on the necessary changes—required capability building and resources, as well as a timeline to get it done.

3. It enables you to stay ahead of your listeners. Karen, a senior manager and a friend from a major consulting company, once told me, "An agenda makes you look more credible because it shows you put in some real thought beforehand." Asked to elaborate, she continued by saying that many people have the urge to be the know-it-all before meetings. However, due to the heavy workload, it is virtually impossible to anticipate all of what is to come during the week. She gave an example of a meeting with an HR VP of a client she served. In this meeting, she carefully split the agenda into what she knew and what she needed to know. She thought hard about what the client wanted, and because she had already noted the issues she knew less about, she was able to ask questions outright. She said, "Having thought through and putting that on paper gives you the right to be not scared about the unknown." Later, her client commended her for being up front and clearly structured.

However, too much stiffness on your agenda and structure can sometimes weigh you down. In this type of sensitive situation, you need to make a quick executive decision. This decision is called releasing your agenda. It occurs when everyone, and especially the key client stakeholder, is not on board. Without buy-in from these participants, any next steps fall on deaf ears. Trust your sixth sense. While you may be eager to lead the discussion your way, you need to learn to be both the presenter and the observer—to be in the room and outside at the same time. If you detect that the outlined process is not clicking, rather than leveling your way in, step back and hear the truths out. Simply ask, "What should we be really discussing at this moment?" Be prepared to let go of your agenda sometimes.

PRINCIPLE 35 Create "Four Boxes" To Dos

What is the best way to keep your everyday "to dos" organized?

One of the most important habits I acquired during my early apprenticeship days was to follow a particular principal who always

Current work – [today's date]	This week new engagements
• Send out e-mails to list of people—add three more to list • Write structure out and categorize • Finish up two more articles (H) • Download framework from research portal • Capability courses • Transfer data to hard drive • . . .	• Ask assistant to get new phone number • New computer (Lenovo?) • Business plan for new school • Generate more cross-border ideas • Read more about finding the right editors and publishing channels
Personal (incl. fitness)	**New learning**
• Book musical tickets for trip to London • Book dinner (noon) two good restaurants • Fix Visa problems • Continue mini-triathlon workout routine • Bring back weekly tennis practice • Birthday present for wife • . . .	• Read more books on influencing others and changing minds • Go out and talk to 15 other new faces within the next two months • Copy some text of great writers • . . .

FIGURE 3.2: "Four Boxes" To Dos

kept four different sections of "to dos." He was a senior principal who was an expert organizer of things. He never missed client meetings and rarely had to shift prescheduled calls around. Moreover, he would send out e-mails to the team to prepare birthday gifts for another team member three weeks in advance. What enabled him to do this was a powerful four-box to do chart (Figure 3.2). The four boxes split in the following way: current work, personal, this week new engagements (for future work), and new learning.

The "four boxes" is powerful because the left-hand side focuses more on the present and ongoing activities and the right-hand side on the future. Splitting that future into two buckets has clear benefits as well. As you start getting involved in different work you tend to lose focus on where your development needs are. By making it vertical top and bottom you are easily able to reflect back and forth to align whether the projects you are working on are in line with your learning goals.

The personal bucket is also highly important (bottom left-hand side). I have emphasized fitness in parentheses to remind myself of the importance of ongoing exercise. Try to include jogging as well as some other form of exercise. You can also remember to write down important family events such as bringing flowers home for a surprise celebration.

The organization of the four boxes is easy and intuitive. It is just a reminder to keep up-to-date on different dimensions so you do not forget important actions. Therefore, when you see empty space in the new learning section, for example, it may be a wake-up call for lack of structured growth. Try to review this every week and update it by drawing a line through the items completed. Do not overload the current work section with details of immediate to dos. That should be saved for your daily notebooks.

You can carry this paper around in a clear file and take it out every week. As Warren Buffett once suggested regarding his investments: "Make it a rule to come back every year to assess your successes and failures of your chosen stocks against your targets." Rather than annual assessment, you should assess your target reached on a weekly basis.

Lastly, create to dos before the start of the day. A lot of people sit down in the morning to create to dos in their office. That is a waste of time.

PRINCIPLE 36 Focus on Outcomes Not Activities

Try remembering the last time you asked yourself, "Was I being productive today or just being active?" Another way to say this is, "Was I closing to dos or just doing things?" How can we become even more vigilant on our accomplishments? Needless to say, leaders are measured on the amount of work accomplished and the subsequent impact that work generated, both in the short and long run.

This is where the principle of *Check in* and *Check out* policy comes in. It is a well-known theory to most McKinsey leaders, especially because many of us have done at least one operation-related client project. It's easy and fast: *check in* with your team before the day starts and *check out* before it ends (or around 5 to 6 P.M.) for just 10 minutes. This method forces you to focus on *outcomes* rather than *activities* during the day. It's imperative that you learn and implement this early because it allows you to free up your own time and spend time working on urgent requests. Excellent leaders focus on several areas and read certain cues during this process. Here is how it works.

Each day, you huddle around to quickly update what will happen during the day. Typically, the junior team members communicate to the engagement manager or other leader how their day will pan out.

1. What is the objective of the day in terms of key deliverables and outcomes?
2. Discuss only *what* and not the *how*, and take *how to* offline in a separate problem-solving meeting as necessary.

By using check-ins, the leader is able to see whether staff members are on top of their work. It helps the individuals practice synthesizing their thoughts since the rhythm is in a more bullet-point form. When getting a download from the team, only allow for a few minutes to understand. If the explanation starts to get long, say, "Okay, let's move on to what we want done." You need to be strict and somewhat by the book. This is not a happy merry-go-round time. It's time to get stuff done, and this is what you need to get across.

Also, realize that *what* and *how* are two totally different discussions. *What* talks candidly about the tasks to be completed and is end-results oriented, while *how* refers to the process. I have tried implementing this in many client contexts, and many have complained of time overrun, hence wasting valuable work time. The de facto reason is due to irrelevant problem solving at that time. Leave that for another discussion. Your credibility as a leader increases significantly when you learn to structure conversations in different domains and keep *what*, *how*, and *why* discussions separate.* Another benefit of focusing on *what* is identifying complications early. You are able to do some heavy lifting on a particular topic faster.

At 5 P.M., before parting, you need to discuss how the day will end using check-outs. Typically, at this time, you ask a few questions:

1. What are the end-of-the-day deliverables? This question focuses on prioritization.
2. When will you receive those deliverables? This question focuses on hard deadlines and incorporates editing and proofreading time.
3. What are the open issue items? This question invites forecasting and prediction of the rest of the week.

A healthy team must respect individuals' time. Therefore, having a set time, such as at 5 P.M., to determine where someone can work is important, if you have additional work. This way you can go to dinner as a team. Or, you can divide up, and dine separately. Sometimes you have out-of-town friends you want to meet instead. This is not possible without a simple policy. Although at first you may not be used to managing someone else's time, this method will force you to become respectful of others. I remember the opposite case. I worked with a certain leader who did not respect time. He would just keep working without even a proper meal and expected

---

* *How* discussions should be done during problem-solving time. *Why* discussions are overarching and broad and should be done early in your project or goal. After this, one should not waste too much time on the *why*.

his team members to do the same. It's a situation you want to avoid. Also, checking out alleviates the anxiety of team members who may be thinking, "Am I on track? Should I be prioritizing X instead of Y?"

At this point it is important to have the details of the deliverables. Oftentimes the biggest issue the next day comes from differences in expectations. Make sure you get the detailed output image. If you are busy due to meetings, ask your team members to write those end-of-day deliverables on the whiteboard or send an e-mail to you.

Occasionally, depending on the type of industry or function you are in, such as a project management office, purchasing and supply chain operations, retail operations, and so on, you need to keep track of all the open issues diligently. Use a spreadsheet and work as a team to check all open issues every week. Open issue tracking should have items such as current work stream, start and due dates, department, topics, and owners.

PRINCIPLE 37 Know Your Meeting Modes in Advance

Categorizing meetings in advance can get you a long way. Over the years, I have categorized the various types of meetings to help set up my meeting modes and to monitor the balance of meetings. Some major categories of meetings are update meetings, alignment/escalation meetings, knowledge sharing and idea generation meetings, and problem-solving meetings. These meeting types, which are outlined in Figure 3.3 in a two-by-two matrix, can be one guideline to help you think about what types of meetings you are spending most of your day in.

Usually, a problem-solving meeting is a decision and directional meeting requiring high complexity. It results in high value. Knowledge-sharing and idea generation meetings, where you invite

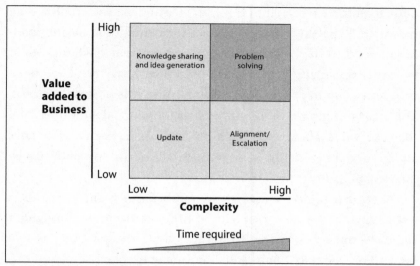

FIGURE 3.3: Types of Meetings

experts from different departments or share mystery shopping results, are a great way to learn something new or expand your existing plans. Alignment and escalation meetings are tricky and highly complex but do not add much value to the business. You need to pay attention to get everyone aligned before the meeting rather than during it. Update meetings are usually low in value and should be avoided if at all possible by using a different communication channel. Out of these four meeting categories, forcing yourself not only to see the current situation but to focus more time and attention on problem solving is imperative.

Previously, in a frontline retail operations project, we went down to the shop floor and did an interesting exercise: we counted the minutes of what staff members actually did. Often we split those behaviors into three categories: idle or time wasted, incidental, and value adding. For example, in one fresh produce section we tracked how much time was spent unloading the goods, neatly putting them in order, checking and updating price tags, loading potentially outdated produce back into the cart, chatting, and so on. Idle time meant staff chatting with colleagues, incidental time meant pushing the cart to the fresh produce section, and value adding would be neatly organizing the produce. A similar study has been done time and again in coffee making to optimize this process in stores. The aim is to get rid of idle time, streamline incidental time, and increase value adding as much as possible in each individual's actions and interactions. In a typical analysis, you can optimize by 20 or 30 percent.

For regular project meetings, we rarely do such analysis. This is unfortunate since we spend a lot of time on meetings throughout the day—some as short as 15 minutes and others as long as two hours. For example, I have gone into many problem-solving meetings where our original aim to find solutions became, instead, to fill in updates for senior leaders. I should have either (1) given that individual a predownload of information via e-mail beforehand or (2) omitted him from the meeting for this occasion. Because I did neither, I ended up wasting everyone else's time. You need to know what meeting mode you want to be in and how you will achieve that goal. If you know that the meeting is about alignment, you should do your homework of prealignment with some key stakeholders beforehand.

When you have time, quickly prioritize current meetings for this week and next week. Learn to jot down which ones are key problem-solving meetings and which ones are not so useful. Cancel or push back meetings that are unnecessary. If an e-mail update will suffice, go for it. You will be able to cut down probably 20 percent of the meetings you have on your plate, especially if you have many senior leaders or bosses on this particular project. Next is to delegate some meetings to other people—be very mindful of which meetings you will attend. By categorizing your meetings clearly, your decision-making will be that much easier.

PRINCIPLE 38 **Proactively Manage E-mail Communication Using the 5D Rules**

E-mails are seductive. Especially at work where the sources of fun are limited, it's a great distraction. The more you do, the more you get seduced. It's inefficiency masked in the disguise of valid work. Therefore, it's imperative you have well-grounded rules. I use the 5Ds—delegate, delete, defer, deword, deactivate.

- **Delegate e-mail writing whenever possible.** How valuable is your time? Honestly, close your eyes and think about it for a second. According to the McKinsey Global Institute (MGI) July 2012 report, our economic and social think tank writes, "[In 2012] the average knowledge worker spent 28 percent of her work time managing e-mails." That means out of a 12-hour day, you are writing e-mails for 3.4 hours. Sounds unbelievable? My guess is that an average consultant spends way more, maybe close to 5 hours a day. So how many e-mails can we write in a day? According to a *Fortune* magazine report, Baydin, an e-mail analysis and management company, shows "the average e-mail user writes 40 messages a day." That's probably too many to write anything meaningful. That roughly calculates out to less than five minutes per e-mail. But we know less is more; focused effort leads to higher quality. As you transition or think about a leadership role, you also need to stop reacting and writing e-mails whenever you get pinged and start delegating. Find a trusted team member who needs both training and a place to shine to write some important e-mails. Find team assistants whose job description is communication and correspondence to help manage schedules *every* time. Some people believe setting logistics is a manager's job, but that is only when it's unavoidable—when if that particular meeting falls through your head is on the line. Otherwise, avoid logistics as much as possible.

- **Delete all trivial e-mails en route.** The time you spend traveling on business trips and the daily commute to and from work is precious. You need to use it wisely. If you are tired, taking a power nap is essential; otherwise, spend your time deleting e-mails.

  This will save you a lot of time in the long run. It will also make you feel great and efficient about work. The concentration of your effort should be on trivial e-mail actions and not reading e-mails, unless they are very urgent. According to *Fortune*: "An analysis of 5 million e-mails from Baydin, an e-mail management service, said the average e-mail user gets 147 messages per day and deletes 71 (48%)." A clean inbox not only frees up space, which is necessary because nowadays companies including McKinsey have automatic deletion in process after hitting a certain mailbox size, but because it is easier to search for important messages.[1]

- **Defer jumping onto e-mails.** There are some e-mails that are fun to write. If your mentee e-mails you, for example, you want to write back to him or her. If your best friend from university writes to you, it's instinctive that you want to jump on it. Although it is fun and you will feel accomplished after writing back to them, you will quickly find yourself left in a puddle of guilt. In these situations, where you don't want to ignore responding to e-mails, it is important to have a "defer" mindset. What I usually do is move that e-mail to a specific inbox folder (or just forwarding it to yourself and sorting under your name later works just as well). Create the necessary time in your day or the week to get back to those e-mails.

- **Deword your e-mails.** After you finish writing each e-mail and while checking for common spelling errors or typos, also add in a "dewording" habit. It's very simple: take out any unnecessary words that don't have any meaning. Some obvious ones are phrases such as "in order to," "as a matter of fact," and "whether or not." For starters reread the classic writing rules book *The Elements of Style*, by E. B. White and William Strunk, Jr.

- **Deactivate e-mails on Friday night and don't open them until your set time.** This is by far the hardest to execute. We are now constantly connected to the Internet, which makes it so *convenient* to check up on our e-mails, especially for work. State-of-the-art tablets, iPhones, and other gadgets make the experience enjoyable as well. Then there is a rise in expectation. We are expected to respond 24-7. We can't even imagine a world now without e-mails and mobile phones. Studies have consistently shown that the level of wait tolerance in people is significantly decreasing: wait anxiety is a huge issue. However, to be efficient and effective means to have rules that work. A general rule of thumb is to check e-mails—or at least respond to them—only on Sunday night. If not, remember it's not the e-mail that's the problem.

PRINCIPLE 39 Speak Up as Early as Possible

Speaking up in a meeting is very important.

At McKinsey you need to speak up at every occasion: team internal problem solving, small client meetings, and large workshops. If you don't speak up, you can expect a quick word from senior leaders on the very first day of the project. They'll say you are not adding any value.

But not everyone is the main content holder. You may not be an expert in the field. Or, you may know little about the context. Or, you may have just joined the project a few days ago. Whatever the case, as you are present in the meeting, you need to find ways in

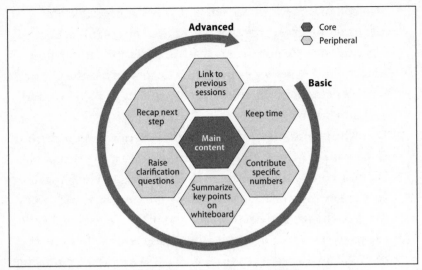

FIGURE 3.4: Peripheral Activities That Allow You to Speak Up

which you can contribute. The secret I've found is focusing on the *peripheral area* surrounding the main content (Figure 3.4). There are six peripheral activities in total: keeping time, contributing specific numbers, summarizing key points on the whiteboard, raising clarification questions, recapping the next step, and linking to any previous encounter with the subject or people.

- **Keeping time** is the most basic activity you can do that actually adds great value when there's a lot of ground to cover. Because other parties may be deeply involved in the content or do not want to get distracted by time, you can play the role of making sure you get through all of the necessary inputs of the meeting.

- **Contributing specific numbers** is a trick done by many smart people. Since it is almost impossible for senior leaders to remember all the numbers, you can help them out by knowing or memorizing key percentages, breakdown numbers, or detailed steps to a process.

- **Summarizing key points** on the whiteboard is one of the best and easiest ways to show presence. You stand up and take down what is being discussed on the table, and after the discussion has relaxed a bit, or the discussion has gone through five or six major points, you can stop to get everyone's attention and thoughts aligned. This is not only extremely helpful for the participants but also a great practice to understand your own grasp of the issues.

- **Raising clarification questions** can be done as a follow-up for key points. Just watch out for unclear objectives or output. Some may only have activities but no real target or goals set. On other occasions, you can quickly enter a heated discussion by saying things like, "Could you elaborate that point?" or "Would you mind sharing some examples?" This is one way to get traction.

- **Recapping of the next step** is usually done by the main content holder. Therefore, it is not necessary unless the meeting finishes without the next step being determined. More often than not, however, you will find that next step is forgotten. To enable yourself to take lead at the right time, you need to listen and constantly be aware of what is missing from the current discussion. Make sure the next step is stated clearly.

- **Linking to a previous encounter with the subject or people** is also a way to add value without knowing the main content. At McKinsey, senior directors add significant insights based on cross-industry implications. A client may be deeply impressed how Coca-Cola's marketing strategy applies to the pharmaceutical industry. It is a more advanced level of action to acquire and also shows a high level of sophistication and credibility.

As mentioned in the opening statement, speaking up is very important. It gives you credibility. It earns you trust not only from your team but from your clients. It builds confidence that permeates into other areas of your work. The one major caution is not to equate loudness with meaningfulness. These six peripheral areas will help you increase your visibility and exposure, but you need to remind yourself to really think before you say anything. A good general rule of thumb is what my mentor and leader of the German commercial vehicle practice Philipp once said to me: "Focus on bringing in perspective and not just your thought. Perspective brings in an angle that leads to decision making, which allows you to add value." Therefore, remember that even in the peripheral area you need to share perspective as much as possible.

As an aside, there is another definition of "speaking up" that means to "raise the issue" at McKinsey. In this case, all it means is that you should not wait until the last critical moment to voice your disagreement or your views on sensitive subject matter. It is a similar meaning to the phrase "obligation to dissent" that I mentioned earlier.

PRINCIPLE 40 Create a Minimalist Presentation Tool Kit

Let me explore with you six crucial slides that have a strong influence on any presentation output I create. These particular slides may not be applicable to everyone. However, having a standard set of templates always helps. These examples are filtered from a list of "enablers" based on the criteria of "core building block material" for a McKinsey presentation.

1. What are the background, issues, and objectives?
2. What changes are we bringing?
3. What are the impacts to be quantified?
4. What are the key questions to be answered?
5. What are the key workshops and meetings within the detailed work plan?
6. What is the proposed project team setup?

A presentation serves the purpose of communicating a message, extending an argument, or testing your hypothesis, among many others. These six core slides are helpful because they can create the general backbone of such as presentation.

BACKGROUND, ISSUES, AND OBJECTIVES (BIO)

Many people frequently forget to give context at the start of presentations. This happens because the context has become part of them already—they've been working "in the zone" for too long and they forget that others know nothing about what they are doing.

Create a "background, issues, and objectives" template to give context to whatever you do. Whether it is to explain the current situation, current complications, or a short background history, it is important to start your presentation with a meaningful context. To accomplish this, we put our understanding of the context on the left-hand side and then what we intend to do on this project—the objectives—on the right-hand side. It's logical to represent the past on the left and the future on the right. Forcing yourself to convey your message in a few bullet points requires practice. This synthesizing effort has a large payoff, though. Listeners can't go beyond three or four large-font bullet points or they lose interest. Think from an audience point of view: it's usually just, "Tell me the big problem and what you are going to do," then get on with it. Your job is to explore the granularity of the problem or context in subsequent chapters.

CHANGES WE BRING

Having a "changes we bring" template works especially well in transformation projects. We call this the "from" and "to" model. The template has "from" and "to" columns that show the current state and the desired future state. It's a quicker way to show the end state: where do we want to finish? At the leadership or board level, swiftness and agility count. It's also a precise way to synthesize all of your learning (if you carried out interviews, field research, analysis, etc.) into five or six bullet points. Drafting an ideal state, the Emerald City, makes sense for anyone. Listeners appreciate this approach because it gives a big picture.

But something easy to understand may be difficult to create. As the famous quotation from President Woodrow T. Wilson goes, "If I am to speak for ten minutes, I need a week for preparation; if fifteen minutes, three days; if half an hour, two days; if an hour, I am ready now." It is a demanding challenge to carefully construct an understandable and thought-provoking message.

NUMBERS TELL THE STORY

As consultants we speak in numbers. If it's a productivity enhancement, we speak in percentages. If it's fixing the inventories and store sales, we speak in turnover ratios. Numbers tell the truths that words may lie about. Without numbers, it's difficult to objectively assess where to play, where to win, and how to win—in a strategy playbook, for example. Numbers are the backbone of any presentation and should be included with an end output image early on. Using a "numbers tell the story" template, you are going to tell the audience, "These numbers are what you are going to find out." Force yourself to "dummy" out a couple of impact calculation slides. By doing so, you bring forward the analysis you need to complete. Aligning this end state with other senior leaders early on can prevent you from chasing after the wrong goal. One time, on a project with a major multinational manufacturing company, I discovered in the first week that the target market was a lot smaller than prior estimates showed. The method was simple. In order to calculate the impact of our investments (ROI), I needed to have a market base. That market base turned out to be only a fraction of what we had thought before. The numbers told us: Don't pursue this track. We were able to quickly shift our client work elsewhere.

KEY QUESTIONS TO ANSWER

The key five to six questions on a "key questions to answer" template should structure your overall document. These questions should clearly link back to your objectives (shown on the first BIO template), so you need to have consistency. Let's say one of your objectives was "to come up with the right operating model." Then in this question section, you would need to address this, for example by saying, "What are the potential combinations of operating models to fit your future growth plans?" or "What are some competitor benchmark references?" Some people have asked me what ties a presentation together in a lucid way. The short answer, I've discovered, is the main questions and subquestions. That's because framing a question requires a deep mental effort—it's challenging.

Consider the subtle but major effect that framing a question can have on you and your audience. For example, let's examine the following three questions:

- Do you want your company's decision-making body to be more in control or less?
- Do you want your company to give more power to subsidiaries?
- Which operating model, a centralized model or decentralized model, do you want to establish?

See how I have framed the questions differently to ask the same question? The first one is skewed toward more control. Every decision-making body would rather have more control than less. The second one is slightly slanted to put you in favor of giving power to subsidiaries. The last one is fair and balanced—the question you should be asking if you want a "non-question-biased" answer.

In recap, key questions help you structure your presentation better. When asking any question, you need to keep in mind what you are trying to frame.

MASTER WORK PLAN

Gantt charts, a bar-type project scheduling format developed by Henry Gantt in the early 1900s, were nonexistent in my work before joining McKinsey. I thought visualizing a work plan was a waste of time. But I was wrong. There are things you can't see in a column-and-row-based Excel sheet. That dawned on me when I was on a product development engagement. Product development or launch is concerned mostly with two things: excellent collaboration among functions and creating a vivid master plan. The "master work plan" template is like a Gantt chart, just in more detail. What's more, it shows you the critical path to project completion. By definition, *critical path* means the least amount of output or the most efficient means required to get to your final destination. A critical path is necessary when making anything because it allows you, by completing necessary prerequisites, to transition from one stage to another. In other words, it focuses your tasks. At McKinsey I learned that visualizing a work plan by showing key meetings, workshops, and milestones allowed everyone to share the same view of the process. Sharing this vision in an easy and understandable way is the nonreplaceable effect of having a master work plan or Gantt chart.

A Gantt chart is usually split into three areas: a description of activities, a timeline (on the upper part), and a person or team that is responsible. On the timeline, you place markers to show important meetings, workshops, and other milestones. Make sure you show the dependency—tasks that must be completed before other tasks can begin or prerequisites of the activities—just like you would see on a product development critical path timeline.

PEOPLE SETUP

Projects have stakeholders. Organizing responsibility and roles up front using a "people setup" template will align the expectations of these individuals. The ingredients that make up a good people setup are a well-defined hierarchy of participants both external and internal to your particular project, role and duty expectations, and governance policy or KPIs. After the team structure is completed you need to align the output with individuals, forcing you to remove any unnecessary people on the team or add people if needed.

In summary, use these templates to help you get started on your presentation material. Then create your own version of a minimalist tool kit of BIO, changes we bring, numbers tell the story, key questions to answer, master work plan, and people setup. I have also kept the number of bullet points below seven because anything above seven ideas, concepts, or sentences is harder for the human brain to digest all at once. This is especially true when you conduct an analysis and present it on a bar chart. We watch out to make sure there are not too many uncategorized, meaningless classifications. Limit your points, questions, or other information into seven points per slide, if possible.

PRINCIPLE 41 Create an Easy-to-Use Template for Updates

Updates take time. But they are a necessary evil. You don't want to be spending too much time, though, because they don't really add much value to you (see "Know Your Meeting Modes in Advance" earlier in this chapter). London School of Economics cofounder and famous playwright George Bernard Shaw said, "The single biggest problem in communication is the illusion that it has taken place."[2] Updates are those hidden traps. Make sure you have an easy-to-use and deliver method so you stay on top.

On numerous occasions in my career, I have witnessed young engagement managers dig holes by forgetting to involve senior principals in advance. What makes it more cumbersome is that McKinsey has a structure that invites sideline leadership (called the Co-ED, or co-engagement directors, for example). Sometimes these participants are invisible. Other times they really want to be involved. It's hard to predict. I'm sure this happens everywhere, in any type of function or industry.

Thus, it is beneficial to create a ready-made template. Have it as a weekly item on your calendar. Even if there is already a typical alignment mechanism such as a 20-minute alignment call with your senior leader in charge, it's definitely not a wasted effort to make sure the update is available. If you are working on many projects at the same time, it's even more effective to have this rule in place.

Here is how the e-mail layout looks like for me. First I start with the overall update. Then, content update. Then I have feedback on client interactions (or customer interactions) and team progress. Finally, I wrap up with some key next steps. Again, your main objective is to hedge any communication inadequacy risk; keep it short and clear.

You can begin your e-mail with something like "Dear XYZ, We just finished our core client meeting and everything went well. Below are some highlights." Then for each section, you may consider writing the points in bullet form using the following guidelines:

Content section:
- Content can be split into key findings and key questions.
- Make bullet points and use short sentences between.
- Usually, three to five key findings and a few key questions, if needed, will do.
- Focus on any new and exciting finding and make sure to *italicize* or **bold** to accentuate the point.

Interactions:
- Report about all the *main interactions you've had this week that the leaders don't know about.*

- Think through your key client counterparts and meetings you have led in a smaller circle. What were some personal concerns, issues raised, and potential opportunities?
- Here, it is important to keep in mind what senior leaders want to know about—not only for the project success of this particular case but also suggesting potential avenues for new value creation.

Team progress:

- Team progress is not about how the team is doing, although this may be important if the project is doing very poorly. Instead, this section should *discuss individual team members' strengths and development needs*, and what leaders can do to help accelerate their growth.
- This weekly update also helps you in your feedback session when you finish your project. It also enables you to raise the red flag earlier should you need help.

Next step:

- Include major dates and deadlines you want the leaders to be aware of. Make them mark them down (although these dates should already be in their calendars) because you want them to know these are of highest priority.
- Sometimes it's beneficial to inform assistants as well as leaders about the next steps.

Always keep e-mails in a simple format with the same structure. Commit to your senior leaders that you will do this every week to force yourself. Stick to that rule. The commitment will help you get clear guidance. I usually try to avoid late nights and choose to write these e-mails in the quiet mornings or when I take the necessary stepping-back time. In many cases, these updates turn into fruitful discussions over concerning issues.

Also, start paying particular attention to short e-mails you write from now on—to your colleagues and friends. A senior principal said it is especially important when writing introduction e-mails to avoid appearing too "friend-like." Introducing one contact to another person, in situations where one is your friend, can make you get sloppy or careless in your writing and structure. Learn from others who do it well. How does this friend depict you? How many words or lines does he use? Does he convey the right message with the audience in mind? Remember to convey professional presence in e-mails when it's appropriate to do so.

CHAPTER FOUR

Going the Extra Mile

Change before you have to.
—JACK WELCH

Perhaps the most noteworthy takeaway from McKinsey, from an organization's perspective, is the importance it places on *iterations*: the systematic process that calls for everyone to not only contribute to produce an end outcome but also to synthesize the best possible one, a bit similar to the wisdom-of-the-crowd concept that the "right answer" can be better derived by combining thoughts from as many people as possible. At the core is one belief: high-impact work comes from believing your output can be iterated repeatedly. For example, we are regularly asked the questions, "Did you run this by XYZ?" when XYZ may not be a direct part of a particular project team. While for some people, this type of iteration may be taken as a nuisance—i.e., more work—at McKinsey, most think it's an extremely positive thing. This attitude and belief makes the Firm distinctive. Not surprisingly, successful entrepreneurs say the same thing. Iteration breaks down wild imaginations and shows you what's going to work instead. McKinsey leaders, entrepreneurs, and corporate CEOs have all learned that iteration is actually the shortest way to produce long-lasting outcomes.

The final section explores more challenging principles: you need to push the extra mile to create your new leadership profile.

The Challenge to Achieve Lasting Growth

Here are the final six principles:

PRINCIPLE 42
Give Away Knowledge and Tools Unsparingly.. Put the "pay it forward economics" in full throttle to make others successful around you.

PRINCIPLE 43
Get Rid of Your Physical Barriers. Tune into your physical constraints that are pulling you back from reaching your full potential.

PRINCIPLE 44
Ask the Second Order Questions. Learn about the deep questions.

PRINCIPLE 45
Learn to Write Fewer Notes Enhance your memory by practicing writing fewer words and retaining more information, just as senior leaders do it.

PRINCIPLE 46
Prepare to Renew Your Life. Become resilient, adaptable, and forgiving toward both the changes you want and the changes that are inflicted upon you.

PRINCIPLE 47
Create Your Own "Profile" as a Leader. Know the ultimate requirements for you to become a leader.

PRINCIPLE 42 Give Away Knowledge and Tools Unsparingly

McKinsey invited an external speaker, Tal Ben-Shahar, a well-known Harvard lecturer in positive psychology, to a weeklong training function in Cambridge, England. Roughly 600 engagement managers from across the globe gathered to join this event, which was a Firm recognition for reaching the first milestone of leadership. In the lecture, Ben-Shahar shared the six different contributing factors to achieving happiness.* One, the spirit of "giving/volunteering," reminded me of how important that had been throughout the past many years at the Firm.

When you join the Firm as a business analyst or associate, one of the first things you learn is the concept of reaching out. Junior consultants reach out extensively to senior leaders because they don't have much of the needed functional expertise or industry experience. At first, everyone is a bit hesitant and skeptical of whether the message will get across, let alone reap any meaningful response. But soon enough, and surprisingly fast, the consultants all experience quick and valuable responses from senior leaders and experts. It's the "pay it forward economics" embedded into the culture of McKinsey—you help others and *others help others*—that has really helped the Firm succeed. This giving and caring mentality encouraged me to follow suit. So during the first year, I also decided to share tools and training materials I had accumulated with many of my office BA cohorts. I compiled neat frameworks in different functions and industries to help expedite the chart creation process for my colleagues. For instance, I shared process flow or value-mapping

---

* To reach a healthy state of happiness, Ben-Shahar stated that an individual should have the following: (1) future goals, (2) ongoing giving/volunteering, (3) an optimistic outlook, (4) identifiable role models, (5) a strength-focused approach, (6) physical exercise at least three times a week (lecture at EM College, University of Cambridge, July 2013).

charts in different detail. I also sent around Excel financial models that I had worked hard on for many days. I knew some coworkers appreciated these because they asked for more individually. Also, for fun, I went out of the way to collect different icons of meeting tables, cool stick figures, and whatnot for use in presentations. Later this blossomed into everyone sharing many different tips, from interview guidelines for different purposes to executive summaries—of course, after sanitization of materials.

In a competitive environment, where you are seeking to get ahead of others, it usually does not make sense to give away privileged materials—you may have the danger of losing your edge. Especially at McKinsey, where an up or out culture is present, this type of thinking, I originally thought, may be detrimental. However, I was proved wrong. At McKinsey, you quickly learn that sharing knowledge is encouraged. We have an internal knowledge database platform that enables consultants to share a range of information, from one-page knowledge nuggets to deep research papers. Spanning over 20 industries and a dozen or more functions, we are able to search relevant professional knowledge and development material at any time. Authors' names are stamped along with other information such as the material's relative shelf life, target audience, permissions, and rights. Consultants and researchers in the Firm upload and contribute to this database as a way of appreciation. When consultants use the term "ramp-up for a study," it usually refers to reading these past documents to quickly gain meaningful background knowledge. The culture that surrounds this platform is a sense of pride rather than obligation. From my experience, when you help others succeed, others—but not necessarily the ones you helped—will help you succeed. Indeed, I still remember a strong senior associate on a particular German automotive study who guided me through the nuts and bolts of direct promotion to associate at the Firm. He kept me up, and he mentored me. He sent me valuable materials that I still use to this day: a structured template to show leaders highlights and development needs. Thanks to his advice, I knew where to focus my efforts very early in my projects. I even knew how the decision committee worked and who was usually involved in the process.

The other benefit of learning the giving mentality is that it dramatically enhances your way for self-improvement. Recall Ben-Shahar from Harvard. During the lecture, he shared with us a story of orphans in the Chicago slums. This misfit group had always been a poor, troubled, and unhappy part of the community who just could not get better. Several attempts to help them failed until a few psychologists went in and had them volunteer to help groups who were even more underprivileged. Then a miracle happened. After these orphans had finished volunteering, they started changing. Their grades became better and their social attitudes changed. The learning was quite straightforward, but the result was extraordinary: when you put yourself out to help people, you learn to help yourself succeed as well. Of course, work life is less dramatic. Yet, when you do start giving and contributing to others, you create a moment of reflection. Since you can't share a bad process flow chart, for example, you learn what best examples look like. In a way, you train yourself to get better at it. By capturing the essence, the next time you are up for a similar challenge, you are ready; you aim higher.

One last bit of advice is how to maximize your giving efforts. Of course, you can first focus on the question of "What adds significant value to people?" but second, also think, "What will add significantly value for me and will also hugely benefit others?" This way, your mind and heart are synced to the effort, helping you make the actions worthwhile, produce better quality, and most important, continue to work at it sustainably. For example, if you are interested in also volunteering outside, rather than just volunteering at an elder care center or teaching underprivileged children, you could try to be a bit more creative. In my case, I joined a group of runners led by a church friend, running to raise money to help a young girl fight cancer. Every weekend we ran, somebody prepared lunch and everyone donated some cash to a fund pool. We were not just running for our own pleasure, but we were also connecting with others. It helped us appreciate health and not take for granted what running means. Try to find a cause and a meaning to give to others. It will help you strengthen your focus and get your desired results.

PRINCIPLE 43 Get Rid of Your Physical Barriers

A recent experienced hire who joined McKinsey Shanghai while his wife lived in Malaysia and his parents, who needed his support, lived in Europe was facing a serious problem: he was underperforming. From the onset, the offer structurally didn't make sense, but that individual still decided to take it. He was set up for failure.

To be successful you need to make decisions to create structural benefits to your life and avoid setting physical obstacles as much as possible. For example, when you are just starting out, at least for the first few years, you should try to live near the office. Should you be working out of the office late at night, a door-to-door of 20 minutes versus 60 minutes makes a huge difference in your sleep time. And sleep deprivation will affect your performance immensely over the long run. Living near the office has many other benefits as well. If you wanted to improve on certain skills or read up on particular subjects, you could afford the extra time to stay later in the office.

You've probably heard the saying, "to be at the right time, at the right place, and at the right occasion"—called TPO for short—many times. That's because most of our successes in life hinge on this saying. So which variable would be the easiest to assert control or influence over? Time would definitely be difficult. Occasion is also something dependent on others. So, by process of elimination, the place—the physical structure—would be the element you would most likely be able to control.

You need to make daily decisions to maximize your long-term benefits. By hiring part-time helpers to clean your house and help you organize things, you can spend more time focusing on networking and skill enhancement. Although this sounds costly, it definitely has its rewards. These minute differences in action can change your life. When looking at the actual execution detail, hiring a helper for a few hours to clean your place up—so that you can do or plan for others things on the weekend—is extremely affordable. James Huang, a successful serial entrepreneur and currently the China CEO of ChannelAdvisor—a NYSE-listed company that provides cloud-based e-commerce management solutions—told me he is very conscious of maximizing his value of time and overcoming as many physical obstacles as possible. He says, "Things will always get in your way; the key is you should always have a laser-focused goal and a way to eradicate x-factors."

It is almost like believing in feng shui, an ancient Chinese mastery that depicts how to balance the energy in your room. In feng shui, written with "wind" and "water" characters, you must explore the natural Taoist rules to place certain things in their rightful place to bring good fortune. You need to engrain a feng shui mindset to achieve your objectives. For example, if you want to focus on your studies, make sure the TV is situated far away from you.

Even within your career, you need to watch out for obvious physical traps and avoid them if you can. My personal experience provides a cautionary tale. I was offered a project in Taiwan that did not have a proper engagement director (the principal in charge of the study). The current engagement director had already been asked to leave the Firm and was actually busy preparing for his next move. The client we were about to serve was also new. Moreover, we had little to no experience across the entire practice to serve this kind of client. On top of this, the other principals involved had stretched their capacity to take on this client—meaning they could not allocate enough time to the project. Lastly, the duration of the study was also cut shorter than usual. In spite of these demanding circumstances, I accepted the offer, thinking I could take on the tidal waves. (I had a streak of great successes until then that made me less careful.) Although we were able to deliver the project to meet or exceed our client's expectations, our team's morale and physical hours, my confidence level, and subsequent internal relationships suffered. Everyone knew it was a bad physical setup, but no one readily admitted it. In the end, the blame was put on me.

Just remember: if you have the right structure in place, you are already a step closer to success. It's really that simple.

PRINCIPLE 44 Ask the Second Order Questions

Consultants, by definition, are client leadership counselors. Therefore, from an early tenure, good consultants develop a question-oriented approach to help clients succeed. Bad consultants, however, typically believe they need to be giving answers all the time or to jump into the teaching mode. Yet, in many cases, executives and client leaders already have a bucketful of answers. Instead, a discovery process must be used to draw these answers out. The top performing senior directors at the Firm have a knack for asking the right question. Tim puts it in a clever way: "You can never teach anyone [at a senior level], but you can [always] help them discover themselves." So what is the right question?

It's difficult to grasp at first, so let's zoom in on an example. Let's say you are helping someone high up make pricing decisions. Normally, what people do is to ask a question pertaining to the factors required to diagnose such decisions. These may be why you want to raise prices, to what level you want to raise them and why, what is the best timing, and so on, basically the "5W1H" questions of who, what, where, when, why, and how. This is called the first order of questions. Although you may be digging into more *whys*, the question still stays in the first order dimension. For example: Why do you want to raise prices? Because the competitor is raising prices. Why is the competitor raising prices? Because the logistic cost is increasing. Why is that increasing? Then you may get to the bottom to justify your decision. It's the standard approach, but it's time consuming and tiring. But there is another, wiser approach to get to the decision. You assume that action, or whatever you intend to question, is already completed. Then ask, what happens next? So you say, "Assuming the prices were raised, then what happens to . . . ? Competitors? Profitability for the long term? Other product lines? Does it still make sense? It automatically enables you to spark interesting conversations and will either deter or encourage your discussion partner with a deeper consequence-driven mind. It also saves the hassle of doing all the analysis and digging beforehand. You try to jump straight to the second order of things. Tim likes to call this thinking a "game theory" frame of mind.

In a strategic game theory mindset you try to think many steps beyond your immediate move. In doing so, you are able to tackle the issue with a wider variety of the solution space. The second order of questions gives you this power.

There are also other ways to help people to think through a different lens. At McKinsey, several leading questions are taught and deployed. Those are:

1. "What if" dream situation questions. These are used for opportunities that may have a different outlook if given a certain condition or context. Examples are:

- Assuming x about the world, what if you were able to change y?
- What if you were given an extra $10 million: what would you do differently?

Usually you can follow this up by asking, "Then, what can you do today that may get you there?"

2. "What you would need to believe . . ." questions. These are used to test out hypotheses or affixed convictions. Examples are:

- What would you need to believe for your company to be selling two times its current revenue?
- What would you need to believe for the bottom 20 percent of your employees to increase productivity?

3. "Standing in the other people's shoes" questions. These are used to identify potential gaps in the current hypotheses or logic by using a similar but different frame. Examples are:

- What would the competitor do if he were in your shoes?
- What would your successor do if he came in and took over your CEO role right now?

4. "Options and alternatives" questions. These are used to put forward alternatives, focusing on the pathway beyond the current suggested options. Examples are:

- You have told me three ways of getting there; how else could we derive the intended outcome?
- What other moves would be better?

This is not an "Option A, B, or C" type of question. These are open-ended questions that force the discussion partner to stretch his or her mind.

5. "Real and practical next step" questions. These lead to concrete steps to achieve goals and help to identify potential roadblocks or risks. Examples are:

- What will get in the way of hiring 100 new employees and letting go 10 percent of the current staff?
- What happens next? Who will be handling this from now on?

Asking the right questions is difficult for anyone. Thus, the ability to do so will let you stand out. These five types of guiding questions should help you start thinking about this topic in the right direction. Try practicing them. Remember, asking thoughtful questions is not based on just having many variations in your brainbox. To ask meaningful and deep questions, you must do three things: first, build experience in the industry or function; second, develop a higher sensitivity to the client, context, or person; and third, try to get to the next order of things as quickly as possible.

PRINCIPLE 45 Learn to Write Fewer Notes

On a project in Montreal, Canada, I met a Chicago-based engagement manager, Kim, who had a very clean notebook with only a few words written for each bullet point. Each page definitely had more white space than ink, making it impossible for me not to catch this interesting phenomenon. From then onward, I observed what we heard in meetings and what she wrote down on paper. For example, we would hear, "Let's have a workshop on February 27, invite three department heads, and spend one hour each on detailed counter-measures, lessons learned, new process flow, required resources and deadline, and drafting the next step proposal and schedule three core meetings for the next two months; participants will be less than 20 people," and Kim wrote down "Workshop Feb 27, detailed proposals, next step." That was it. On the other hand, I was busy capturing many details to minimize the risk of missing points. Then during our internal problem-solving session a strange thing happened. Kim wrote on the whiteboard exactly those words she captured in her note, but spoke of the entire content in detail. I sat there completely stunned. The next day, I happened to attend an important meeting with senior VPs and the CEO with one of the senior directors, Karel, who carried an even smaller black moleskin notebook. Curious, I took a quick glance while he was flipping his pages, and bam, I saw the same brief notes (only a bit messier with cursive writing). Now I knew something was up.

When I asked Kim about this she first smiled, happy to see that I had caught this special technique. She said taking fewer notes is a way to give intensive training for the mind.

First, it not only forces you to remember things, it actually enhances your focus on what is being discussed at the moment. "That is why," she said, "Senior leaders are in the discussions a lot more [than junior members]." Kim also learned early that senior leaders not only had fewer words written per bullet point but also fewer bullet points than she did. At that time, she was trying to train her prioritization skills by learning to weed out "the unnecessary but seemingly important points from the really critical ones."

Second, it helps you to synthesize points clearly. Obviously you will have to test and try, but as you focus on this effort, you will learn certain "buzzwords" that enable you to recall the rest of the dialogue. It's almost like remembering your favorite song verse. When you start singing "Last Christmas, I gave you my heart . . ." from Wham, it inevitably just leads to ". . . and the very next day, you gave it away." It helps to remember that starting buzz line.

Third, it makes it easier for you to communicate your message to others and to tailor to the level easiest for your audience to understand. This enhances your messages' stickiness. For example, it is harder to remember "Complicated product design and feature standards in global markets deter us from entering more in some Chinese cities" than "prevent overengineering when entering Chinese cities," which reduces the original 18 words to only 6 words.

Here are some things you can work on to practice taking fewer notes:

1. First, buy a nice expensive notebook to make you cherish your pages. Make sure you buy a small notebook, but bigger

than pocket size. I usually recommend buying a black leather or moleskin notebook because it has a professional look.

2. Hold yourself accountable early on. Active listening in a group setting is hard, especially if you are not held accountable for it.

3. Use risk-free opportunities to practice. Feedback sessions are great. Trainings are even better. Most companies give training sessions throughout the year, and this is your chance to practice better note taking.

4. Get help from a colleague. Recap key points and share notes from a training or conversation with him or her to see how much "less" you have captured.

5. Give yourself some time to practice and get better at note taking. Throughout our schooling, we are taught to take very "good" notes—which usually means long and detailed notes. Remember, taking fewer notes is about accomplishing better memory retention, listening, and prioritization.

In the long run, a person who takes in only the main points will retain a wider range of information. If you've ever wondered, as I have, why senior leaders are able to juggle so many different topics, business problems, and people at the same time, the solution may be that they are able to compartmentalize more information with fewer words—they only need to hold the "cue" to unlock massive information underneath. Accomplishing the same feat will give you the edge early in your leadership career. Meetings that last over two hours will become bearable because you have mastered taking shorter notes. Just start practicing tomorrow.

PRINCIPLE 46 Prepare to Renew Your Life

Life does not always go as planned. You might have wanted to make a long-lasting career at media but your team captain was a bullying psychopath. Or you wanted to go study abroad, but that year there was a huge riot in your destination country and your parents convinced you it wasn't safe to go. Or you were up for promotion when suddenly the company hired someone external to fill that position. Life is indeed "like a box of chocolates," and you never truly know what is lined up for you, as Forrest from the movie *Forrest Gump* so rightfully put it. But the more amazing thing about life is that *what you might want or desire changes all the time.* That's why it's important to have a mindset that allows you to be more resilient, adaptable, and forgiving toward renewing yourself, whether a change was forced on you or purported by your own will.

Change of self-definition is a good place to start. Did you know that how we define ourselves and relate to things of value changes all the time? For example, just recently, I made an admiring comment to a hugely successful individual. He cotaught at a prestigious university, had published many books, and held a prominent position at a respectable company. I told him that how he managed to simultaneously be successful in so many enterprises was beyond imagination. His reply was, "It's nothing compared to spending time with my kids." He had a genuine smile and a sense of satisfaction when he touched upon his children that made me quickly follow up on that topic instead. Age definitely has a significant influence on your self-definition and worth. For example, when you are in your twenties to midthirties you are predominantly occupied with achieving success in your career, in the fastest way possible. You typically measure your achievements in terms of career success. But as you enter your late thirties to forties, your value may shift to other things such as your family, your interests, and contributions to society. Nearing your midforties to fifties and onward, more emphasis is usually put on your friend network and health. What you want changes. Therefore, how you add value to others and yourself changes with it. And your definition of achievement and success ultimately changes as well.

At each stage of change, one needs to believe that his or her priorities are not strange. There is nothing wrong with a lesser emphasis on career advancements than you had before or more emphasis on pursuing your interests or contributions to society. What's important is to have the ability to *reinvent yourself* once you've realized your mind shift.

At McKinsey, consultants need to reinvent themselves all the time and mostly through personal choice. Some people decide to transfer abroad. Others try to switch roles. Some principals or directors might hop on to a new industry as a big client suddenly decides to go elsewhere or disappears. Whatever the scope and magnitude, the malleability of the individual is being tested. Successful transformers survive and create new paths of their own.

According to a senior director with 20 years at the Firm, there were four major renewals in his career. The first one was when he first arrived in Hong Kong as a business analyst. He wanted to satisfy his insatiable appetite for adventure. The second was during the transition from associate to engagement manager in Europe. This transition from an analyst to manager, he says, "was the most memorable." The third was building the practice from the ground up in China as the cofounding principal and location manager. The fourth one happened four to five years ago. He decided to join the think tank arm of McKinsey to focus more on research and the impact of urbanization in China.

In any case, however, your value is lost quickly during renewal; rebuilding your value in a new context takes time. Therefore it's important to understand what you can control. For example, when the director moved to China (the third shift), he faced several issues ranging from language to local knowledge to being a *laowai* (foreigner). He knew he had limited cards to play with. He spoke Chinese fluently, but yet not to the superior level required to engage deeply with local officials, and he was distanced from the cultural understanding.

He recalls, "I could only focus on one or at most two clients at a time not because I wanted to but because I was limited to." In fact one of his large MNC clients in the aluminum sector materialized only because that CEO showed up. "Most things are uncontrollable," he reminisces, "but you need to make sure you are always adapting." Under the direction of his McKinsey mentor, he actually had to spend two to three years outside of China in the mid-1980s before coming back when China took off. But no matter how hard or how bad the odds were against him, he didn't quit in his renewal.

Therefore be prepared for renewal and reinvention in life. It's normal that expectations change, and what you want changes along with them.

PRINCIPLE 47 Create Your Own "Profile" as a Leader

I cannot end this book without talking about the most important topic of all: ultimately, what kind of attributes, in a nutshell, will determine whether a person will reach a principal-equivalent level? After all, this has been a burning question ever since I started in the business world. And even though I can't speak for the entire industry, I can shed some light on McKinsey and what senior leaders say about the people they think have the potential of being elected.

"What criteria do you look at?" I asked a few senior principals and directors. This is the topic of interest for many consultants, especially senior associate principals in the next promotion window. I still remember the Firm delivering a series of online videos that showcased the entire selection process like a documentary channel. They showed footage of roundtable discussions, interview comments from panelists (you could sometimes guess which candidate they were talking about), and a McKinsey host, who gave the insider look.

From a McKinsey consultant perspective, a potential leadership profile looks into the following four dimensions. Potential leaders must be:

1. **Incredible with other people.** These are people who have an insane amount of energy to inspire and excite other consultants, clients, and leaders. They develop their own McKinsey passion by attracting clients with their "excellent client hand" brand recognition.

2. **Problem-solving maestros.** Words such as innovative, creative, state-of-the-art, high-value-adding, and thought leader fit perfectly to describe these individuals. At the same time, they lay the groundwork and elements of building the Firm into the future problem-solving powerhouse.

3. **Extremely great at getting stuff done.** They are ultimate implementers who have a clear expertise. Clients, consultants, and other colleagues will go to them for guidance on a particular topic. "If it's on X, you go see him," is the perfect description.

4. **Entrepreneurial (in the Firm context).** They take initiative and free will to create something new or take an existing practice to the next level. Like entrepreneurs, they are adept at leveraging, bringing together, and formulating plans from limited resources, human and financial capital, etc.

"People who climb the ladder quickly tend to do exceptionally well along the four dimensions. People who struggle are generally those who are just generally okay with the four dimensions or terribly bad at one thing," one principal said. You must look at it like a bar chart or a diamond-shaped spiderweb. For all four dimensions you need to be above a certain threshold, but typically you need to have a spike in one area.

The four dimensions, I believe, are applicable to all sorts of industries. Many businesses elect leaders based on the abilities to engage people, think outside the box, get things done, and venture into new areas.

I'd like to end with one ultimate question to think about that struck my heart on this journey into the principles of leadership success:

"What are *you* going to bring that will make your place of leadership in the world a *better place* and not just a bigger place?" Leaders become leaders because they bring in something better, different, and indispensable.

CHAPTER FIVE

Become a Thinker and a Writer

I hope you were able to think about more principles as you read along. In Chinese, there is an idiom that literally translates to "raise one and infer three" and means to deduce multiple things from one core idea. The origin comes from Confucius, who told his students that he would not teach them any lessons unless they were able to infer three things from one teaching.

Thinking Sets Leaders Apart

McKinsey hires people who love to think (don't say this if you ever go for an interview, show it!). Thinking is the proof of our existence, as French philosopher and mathematician Rene Descartes so eloquently said, "Je pense, donc je suis (I think, therefore I am)," in *Discourse on Method*, almost 400 years ago. There's so much to learn from this world. Just today, someone taught me the origin behind why we have corporations. Did you know that corporations came from colonial ventures by Dutch and British trading companies such as the Dutch and British East India Company in the early 1600s? The idea was to diversify losses from sinking ships during their risky sea voyages. Because they knew x number of vessels would sink en route, but didn't know which ones, they formed coalitions of shareholders who would own and share equal rights of the entire fleet, or "corporations." This way, interested businessmen could reap the enormous return on investment without making an uncertain bet on a single ship. Or, what about the word *entrepreneurs*? Its origin is French and means to bring something of a lower yield to a higher yield. In other words, entrepreneurs, through their new inventions and innovations, are called so rightfully because they create "additional value," in a literal sense.

In China, the word for *thing* is written with two characters that mean "East West." Why would anyone call it that? Well, contrary to the intuitive belief that trade was vibrant in the East and West parts of the world, it originated in the Tang dynasty when two large commerce and shopping markets called the "Dong (East) Market" and "Xi (West) Market" presided next to each other. At the time, in the old capital of Chang An (current day Shang Xi Province, Xi'an capital), people routinely said they would go buy at the East and West market. This was the birth of an elemental word such as a "thing."

There are many great philosophers and thinkers who have equipped us with the chance to explore more of our minds. However, whatever you know now, you don't know quite enough. That's the truth. You are limited by the capacity of thinking you know. Concepts like "thinking outside the box" that we use regularly are important to train your brain to develop eternal curiosity.

I believe knowledge stems from curiosity. The more curious you are, the more you become aware, and the more you desire to know. For example, you might read in a book, "Innovation is the central job of a leader." Someone like the now-legendary Steve Jobs, the pioneer of Apple's "Think Different" campaign, could have said that. Or, in another article, you may read, "Finding great talent is the central job of a leader." Jack Welch, who constantly said to surround yourself with people who are smarter than you are, might have said that. So, which is more true? Is creating innovation or finding talent the central job of leaders? For both statements you have legendary representatives. Well, probably innovation and talent are both required to become a great leader. Most of the time, it is not the fact or evidence that matters, but association and implications. Realizing this may lead you to become more curious about the style of leadership you want to take.

We are often told to *learn more* while we are growing up. While that's true, the real fun begins when you *think more*—dig to the fundamental layer of thoughts, things, and occurrences, then take their implication and association seriously. Think and learn, learn and think—going around in this circular motion. If you were to single out a commonality among McKinsey consultants and future leaders, again, I believe it will be in their pursuit of thinking. And that's the silver lining for everyone who attempts to put in the time and effort to think about these success principles.

Marvin Bower on the Value of Writing

Before I end this book I want to send you off with one final note from the words of McKinsey's most influential and prominent leader, Marvin Bower. Marvin's thought and relentless adherence to professional standards built the Firm and set enduring values for consultants to follow in the years to come. To this day, he is revered by most consultant colleagues as the founding father of the management consulting industry, most notably of top-management advisory. In one of his books, *Perspective on McKinsey*, which is given to all consultants who enter McKinsey, he writes, "My willingness to [write] so early in the study brought me opportunities to act as engagement manager. . . . Over the years I advised this approach and urged associates to put their ideas about the Firm in writing. Not many [did]. Those who did consider it worthwhile usually had the other qualities of mind and makeup that fitted them for advancement to positions of responsibility." He ends later in the section, "Quality reports are difficult to write, we too often omit them entirely or substitute reproduction of visual aids." In his book, he stresses the importance of writing reports by quoting Mac (James O. McKinsey), one of his early mentors, who said, "Unless they [associates] can write reports that are logical and clear you can be fairly sure that their thinking is murky. I think, therefore, that the report can be used as the most useful instrument for training."

And here lies the essence for your future growth: write your own success principles and put those ideas into a coherent structure with a strong focus on quality. It will be one of the most effective instruments for training your future leadership mind.

As I bulldozed through a few sleepless nights while writing this book, it came clear also to me that putting structure, key takeaways, and immediate actions into each article were arduous and excruciating mental processes. Malcolm Gladwell, the author of *Outliers*, writes that to be an expert at anything you require at least 10,000 hours of practice—practice at the top-gear level. Clive Thompson, a tech correspondent for the *New York Times*, wrote in his book *Smarter Than You Think*, "The act of writing forces [professional writers] to distill vague notions into clear ideas. . . . This is why writers often find that it's only when they start writing that they figure out what they want to say." This rescued me from thinking my writing was always light-years away from my thought—and I had a huge issue with that! Now, I am comfortable taking a few baby steps at a time. Now, I believe writing is something every aspiring person should practice to get better every day. You will reap profound benefits when you have to send that company memorandum to your fellow employees one day. Or, so I'd hope.

APPENDIX I

McKinsey Structure

In general, people who work at the Firm are referred to as consultants regardless of their actual title in the Firm. Since this was a book on leadership transition, however, I have used many internal job titles to facilitate the discussion and give perspective on the success principles. Yet, if you are new to this world, the different titles can become confusing. Thus, I have created a simple hierarchical structure (Figure A.1) to answer the question, "What exactly is each level responsible for?"

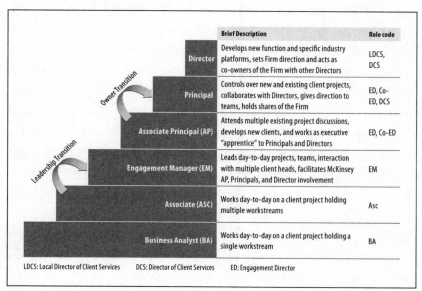

	Brief Description	Role code
Director	Develops new function and specific industry platforms, sets Firm direction and acts as co-owners of the Firm with other Directors	LDCS, DCS
Principal	Controls over new and existing client projects, collaborates with Directors, gives direction to teams, holds shares of the Firm	ED, Co-ED, DCS
Associate Principal (AP)	Attends multiple existing project discussions, develops new clients, and works as executive "apprentice" to Principals and Directors	ED, Co-ED
Engagement Manager (EM)	Leads day-to-day projects, teams, interaction with multiple client heads, facilitates McKinsey AP, Principals, and Director involvement	EM
Associate (ASC)	Works day-to-day on a client project holding multiple workstreams	Asc
Business Analyst (BA)	Works day-to-day on a client project holding a single workstream	BA

LDCS: Local Director of Client Services   DCS: Director of Client Services   ED: Engagement Director

FIGURE A.1: Basic Hierarchical Structure

An Organization Model That Acts as the Success Pillar for the Firm

Consulting sells complex services. McKinsey sells the most premium services of all. Projects that take a few months can cost over a million dollars. Complex services take more time to sell and require highly sophisticated salespeople and channels. This is true especially for the business-to-business (B2B) franchise. For it to be successful, multiple forces must work together, including high brand value, a high-performing culture, top-notch talent, proprietary knowledge resources, a *distinctive organization structure*, and others. Entrepreneurs say there is always a reason why a business succeeds that shows in its business model: how people are able to effectively carry out their given roles. For McKinsey and other consulting companies that followed, I believe, this success has been the result of a lean structure along with its unique problem-solving method, which has been emulated by both other consulting firms and corporations.

Notice that for complex services the salespeople are at the very top instead of at the bottom. It's awkward at first when you realize this dynamic. Especially when you become the engagement manager, to have all the people look to you for specific project ownership and leadership, suddenly you must step up more than just a few steps. As an engagement manager you are nearly forced into a state of "You handle everything" and handed the conductor's baton. As you learn more about the Firm and the top-management consulting industry, you realize that this is quite a lean and effective business model. It makes sense that highly sophisticated conversations are conducted by the most senior, experienced, and trained communication specialists—directors and senior principals. A $2 million high-potential lead is a huge opportunity and must be directed by the best. Thus, consultants never really find out the "sales" function until the very end of their career, and they do so only in its most complex form, which is not the traditional push sales form but by giving clients a reason to say, "Hmm, sounds interesting, do you want to send a proposal about the framework or approach you just mentioned?" Consultants who become savvy at giving the tip-of-the-iceberg answers but not giving away the entire glacier lure in the clients to ask for more. It's a definite skill necessary for complex services. The Firm trains this mental awareness and communication skill for many years, and it is so important that even a person who was a high-level senior executive at another company with 15 years of experience, should he or she choose to join the Firm, will need to go through the entire McKinsey learning process from the associate level, though it would be in an accelerated way. In the mind of every consultant who has experienced McKinsey training, there lies a deep understanding of how leadership development works: first, by beefing up your fundamental skills and capabilities (in this case, problem solving), next, by honing your listening and communication over many years, and finally, by perfecting your mindset and character in the long run (the hardest things to change). Only then will you have the necessary ability to stand in the circle of leaders. Although this book is about leadership transition, it is important for you to understand how your organization is structured and how it should work. Typically, learning about what you sell is a great starting point. Unless you are an entrepreneur, which by definition as founder and CEO entitles you to a leadership position and an understanding of your own business model, most people will need to climb their way up. Thus you need to figure out what forces are at work and how you can be successful in the given position. For example, some McKinsey people leave the Firm after reaching associate principal because they can't master or get accustomed to the newly charged "sales" role. They'd rather look for a prominent mid- to back-office COO leadership path. For an organization structure to work, the people working need to be efficiently utilized. Some organizations do a poor job and create massive management overhead problems because the structure does not fit the nature of their business. For example, if your organization is based on a door-to-door sales model selling kitchen supplies, you don't need many manager-tier people. Instead, you need better training and tools to empower each salesperson and a system that weeds out salespeople who are unfit for the job.

McKinsey's organization model is bound to work given the nature of what it sells. This model also explains why consultants work around the clock. Each consultant, regardless of tenure, is tasked with different roles that can be unbounded. Senior leaders need to keep pushing potential client engagements into the pipeline due to a long lead time or harvesting period. Engagement managers and below need to help clients justify their cost. The only difference is that senior leaders can control their work time as long as they are pulling in their sales quota weight, while consultants need to rely on client expectations that are outside their control.

NOTES

INTRODUCTION

1. These numbers come from multiple sources: Del Jones, "Some Firms' Fertile Soil Grows Crop of Future CEOs," *USA Today*, January 9, 2008, http://usatoday30.usatoday.com/money/companies/management/2008-01-08-ceo-companies_N.htm; Kerima Greene, "McKinsey's 'Secret' Influence on American Business," CNBC, September 13, 2013, http://www.cnbc.com/id/101030774.
2. Yahoo! Finance, ycharts.com/companies/AAPL/market_cap.

CHAPTER 1

1. Mark Hurd, "The Best Advice I Ever Got," during his CEO and chairman position at Hewlett-Packard, *Fortune*, August 4, 2008, accessed January 4, 2014, archive.fortune.com/galleries/2008/fortune/0804/gallery.best advice.fortune/6.html.
2. My discussion on early risers draws on multiple sources, which drew on further sources like AP, *Fortune*, *New York Times*, etc., in each of the websites. I took the information and created a quick table and analyzed the wake-up time of CEOs. The direct websites were from Tim Dowling, Laura Barnett, and Patrick Kingsley, "What Time Do Top CEOs Wake Up?" April 1, 2013, accessed January 8, 2014, http://www.theguardian.com/money/2013/apr/01/what-time-ceos-start-day; Max Nisen and Gus Lubin, "27 Executives Who Wake Up Really Early," January 11, 2013, accessed January 8, 2014, http://www.businessinsider.com/executives-who-get-up-early-2013-1?op=1; Kylepott, comment on Jim Citrin at Yahoo! Finance survey, "The Daily Routine of 17 CEOs," *Lifehack Blog*, accessed January 9, 2014, http://www.lifehack.org/articles/lifestyle/the-daily-routine-of-17-ceos.html.
3. Phil Ament, "Thomas Alva Edison," *The Great Idea Finder*, October 28, 2005, accessed December 28, 2014, http://www.ideafinder.com/history/inventors/edison.htm.

4. Eric Finzi, "How Smiles Control Us All," *The Atlantic*, January 30, 2013, accessed June 22, 2013, http://www.theatlantic.com/health/archive/2013/01/how-smiles-control-us-all/272588/.
5. Ken Eisold, "Unreliable Memory: Why Memory Is Unreliable, and What We Can Do About It," *Psychology Today*, March 12, 2012, accessed August 3, 2015, https://www.psychologytoday.com/blog/hidden-motives/201203/unreliable-memory; Laura Englehardt, "The Problem with Eyewitness Testimony," *Stanford Journal of Legal Studies*, April 5, 1999, accessed August 3, 2015, http://agora.stanford.edu/sjls/Issue%20One/fisher&tversky.htm.
6. Tim Bradshaw, "Lunch with the FT: Brian Chesky," December 26, 2014, accessed Jan 1, 2015, http://www.ft.com/cms/s/0/fd685212-8768-11e4-bc7c-00144feabdc0.html; past discussion with my colleague from Groupon who moved to Airbnb sparked this example; Phil Ament, James Dyson, *The Great Idea Finder*, March 20, 2006, accessed January 28, 2015, http://www.ideafinder.com/history/inventors/edison.htm; Jeff Dyer, Hal Gregersen, and Clayton M. Christensen, *The Innovator's DNA: Mastering the Five Skills of Disruptive Innovators* (Harvard Business Review Press, 2011).
7. Sahoj Kohli, "How walking Can Make Your Brain Healthier—and More Creative," *The Huffington Post*, September 8, 2014, http://www.huffingtonpost.com/2014/09/08/how-walking-improves-your-brain-health-and-creativity_n_5786560.html; Alison Griswold, "To Work Better, Just Get Up from Your Desk," *Forbes*, June 12, 2012, accessed January 10, 2015, http://www.forbes.com/sites/alisongriswold/2012/06/12/to-work-better-just-get-up-from-your-desk/.

CHAPTER 2

1. John Medina, "Attention," *Brain Rules*, http://www.brainrules.net/attention/?scene=1; see also his videos on "A perfect commercial" of Apple's 1984 commercial (video log page: 9/9), or visit YouTube, 1984 Apple's First Macintosh Commercial, https://www.youtube.com/watch?v=OYecfV3ubP8.
2. Stephen E. Kaufman, *The Art of War* (Vermont: Tuttle Publishing, 1996).
3. Stephen R. Covey, *The 7 Habits of Highly Effective People: Powerful Lessons in Personal Change* (New York: Simon and Schuster, 2004), 41.
4. Maya Angelou, *Letter to my Daughter* (New York: Random House, 2008), Kindle edition.
5. Charles Duhigg, *The Power of Habit: Why We Do What We Do and How to Change* (London: Random House, 2012), 129–135.
6. Sheryl Sandberg, *Lean In* (New York: Alfred A Knopf, 2013), 89–90.

7. Robert Keegan and Lisa Laskow Lahey, *Immunity to Change* (Boston: Harvard Business Press, 2009), 14–15.

CHAPTER 3

1. Laura Vanderkam, "Stop Checking Your Email, Now," *Fortune*, October 8, 2012, accessed July 7, 2013, http://fortune.com/2012/10/08/stop-checking-your-email-now/.
2. Marlene Caroselli, *Leadership Skills for Managers* (New York: McGraw-Hill, 2000), 71.

INDEX

ABOUT THE AUTHOR

Shu M. Hattori is a Japanese-British national with experience in management consulting, venture capital, online social commerce, and news media. As an engagement manager in McKinsey & Company, he served in advanced industries, high-tech, and media in Asia, North America, and Europe. He is an applied linguist, a native speaker of Japanese and English, and fluent in Chinese. He cofounded Knowledge Flow, a China-Japan job web portal bridging software engineers, in 2007 and a wedding proposal studio, W2 love, in 2011.

Shu has a passion for learning and professional development. He's been selected to give leadership training for companies and to act as a mentor for McGill students and has been involved with creating young leaders. He hopes to engage more people to believe in their own leadership and breakout potential. Shu earned an MBA from National Taiwan University with a full government sponsored scholarship and a bachelor's degree in commerce with distinction from McGill University in Canada.